AN INDEX TO THE EVANGELIST and THE CHRISTIAN

AN INDEX TO THE EVANGELIST and THE CHRISTIAN

Compiled by

David I. McWhirter
Director of the Library and Archives
Disciples of Christ Historical Society

And by

Dennis Gulledge, Minister
Millidgeville, Georgia

College Press Publishing Company, Joplin, Missouri

Printed and bound in the
United States of America
All Rights Reserved

Library of Congress Catalog Card Number: 83-70079
International Standard Book Number: 0-89900-231-5

INTRODUCTION

And Key to the Use of the Index

by David I. McWhirter

Despite its comparatively short life, the *Evangelist* was influential in the Campbell-Stone Movement. Its editor, Walter Scott, is looked upon as one of the foremost pioneers of the Movement.

The *Evangelist* did not run continuously from 1832 - 1842 but was interrupted for two years. In 1836 Walter Scott published his *The Gospel Restored* as a volume of the *Evangelist* but it is largely considered to be a monograph. In 1837 Scott joined with John T. Johnson in Georgetown, Kentucky, to publish the *Christian*.

This index is for the years 1832 - 1835 and 1838 - 1842 of the *Evangelist and the January - October, 1837 numbers of the Christian*. References to the *Christian* are indicated by the notation '37C in the index in the place of the year.

Only the month, year and page number are cited for articles and subjects in this index. Entries under an author's name are complete with the title of the article. Place names and other aids in identifying subjects and authors are added in parentheses.

Articles by a person appear under the person's name. In these entries the author's name appears in upper and lower case letters. Subjects are indicated by all upper case letters.

With a few exceptions the page cited is the first page on which the subject appears in an article. When locating a cited page the user should check through the remainder of the article for further references to the subject. Once an article ends a new citation is made for the next appearance of the subject.

v

Sears List of Subject Headings is the authority for subject headings. Additional subject headings were used as necessary because of the unique subjects dealt with in this index.

Anyone familiar with 19th Century journalism will realize that spelling, especially of names, was not yet standardized. Names would be cited phonetically so variant spellings appear. Names should be checked under various possible spellings as this index generally lists the name as it appears in the journal.

One should familiarize oneself with special subjects used in this index. Church bodies are listed under the term which applies to members of that body. Some cross references appear in the index to help users locate similar subjects.

It is hoped that errors discovered by users of this index will notify the compiler and the Disciples of Christ Historical Society so that the master file can be corrected.

The College Press reprint edition of The *Evangelist* and The *Christian* was used to compile this index.

INTRODUCTION

And Key to the Use of the Index

by Dennis J. Gulledge

This is primarily a topical index. It is concerned only with the titles of articles in *The Evangelist*. It also covers correspondence which was carried on with and by Walter Scott.

This index does not concern itself with place names and personal names — such as those mentioned in David McWhirter's index. Personal names appear only as those mentioned in correspondence and obituaries.

Dennis J. Gulledge

A

A., D. (Ohio)
Progress of Reform. Feb'34:46

AAIKIN, R. (KENTUCKY)
Jan'37C:23

ABBOTT, W. (KENTUCKY)
Jan'37C:23

ABERNETHY. (KENTUCKY)
Jan'33:22

ABRAHAM (PATRIARCH)
Apr'34:76

ADAIRSVILLE, KENTUCKY
Sep'42:215

ADAM (FIRST MAN)
Apr'32:89
May'32:104
Nov'32:258

ADAMS. (KENTUCKY)
Jul'37C:151
Dec'40:284

Adams. (New York) (Presbyterian)
The influence of personal piety
on pulpit eloquence. Feb'42:
34

ADAMS. (OHIO)
Jan'39:24
Mar'39:72

ADAMS, A. (KENTUCKY)
Jul'37C:151

ADAMS, ABSALOM (KENTUCKY)
Oct(ieSep)'37C:176

ADAMS, D. (KENTUCKY)
Jan'37C:23

ADAMS, JOHN QUINCY
quoted. Jan'40:22

ADAMS, L. (KENTUCKY)
Jan'37C:23

ADAMS, R. (KENTUCKY)
Jan'37C:23

Adolescenes
Caesar vs. the Christian.
Sep'38:197

THE ADVOCATE FOR THE TESTIMONY
OF GOD AS IT IS WRITTEN ON
THE BOOKS OF NATURE AND
REVELATION (J. THOMAS)
May'37C:100,117

AFFLECK, THOMAS
Oct'41:237

AFFLICTION
See
JOY AND SORROW

AKER, PETER (ILLINOIS) (METHODIST)
May'33:110

ALABAMA
Aug'32:192
Dec'33:283
Jun'34:132
Sep'34:216
Dec'34:282
Jul'35:167
Aug'35:191
Jan'39:24
Sep'39:205
May'40:113
Aug'40:190

ALBANY, KENTUCKY
Jan'39:24

Alden, Ch. O. (Kentucky)
Letter. May'40:118

ALGAIER, C. U. (KENTUCKY)
Jan'37C:23

ALLEGHANY CITY, PENNSYLVANIA
Jan'38:9

ALLEN. (KENTUCKY)
Aug'41:190

ALLEN, BEN (KENTUCKY)
Jan'37C:20,21

Allen, Thomas M.
Letter. Sep'33:213
Letter. Oct'39:238
Letter. Nov'39:263
Letter. Jul'40:154
Letter. Sep'40:216
Letter. Apr'41:95
Note. Jul'41:165
Letter. Sep'41:214

ALLEN, THOMAS M.
Jan'40:24
Oct'41:230
quoted. Nov'41:248
May'42:117

ALLEN, TIMOTHY (OHIO)
Aug'33:192

ALLERTON, A.
Jan'38:15

ALLIN, PHILIP T. (KENTUCKY)
Jul'40:148

Alumnus
Jesus. Jan'33:17
Thoughts on Parables.
        no. 1. Feb'34:25
        no. 2. May'34:98

ALUMNUS
Jun'34:121

Amend, William
On the restoration of the Ancient
        Gospel. Jul'33:160

AMERICAN BIBLICAL REPOSITORY
quoted. Feb'42:34

AMERICAN BOARD OF COMMISSIONERS FOR
        FOREIGN MISSIONS
May'33:120

AMERICAN COLONIZATION SOCIETY
May'33:116

AMERICAN REPOSITORY
quoted. Apr'32:96
quoted. Jun'32:144

AMMEN, J. (KENTUCKY)
Aug'37C:167
Oct(ieSep)'37C:183

ANABAPTISM
May'40:112

ANCIENT GOSPEL
Jan'32:8
Feb'32:25

ANDERSON, W. (KENTUCKY)
Mar'34:64

ANDOVER, MASSACHUSETTS
May'33:116

ANDREW, J. O. (METHODIST)
Jun'38:137

ANDREW, J. P. (OHIO)
Sep'33:214

ANDREWS. (KENTUCKY)
Sep'32:215

ANECDOTES
Feb'32:48   Sep'38:209
Jul'32:160   Mar'39:69,71,72
Sep'32:207   Dec'39:279,280,2
Jan'33:3   Mar'41:68
Mar'33:59   Jul'41:161
May'33:116   Aug'41:188,189
Nov'35:263   Oct'41:221
Jan'37C:6,7,8   Jan'42:13
Jan'38:20

ANGELS
Apr'38:91

ANGER
Dec'39:279

ANTI-CHRIST
Feb'32:42

ANTIOCH, KENTUCKY
Jan'39:23
May'42:117
Jun'42:139

ANTIOCH (CALLOWAY CO.) MISSOURI
Nov'39:263

ANTIOCH (RANDOLPH CO.) MISSOURI
Nov'39:264

ANTIOCH, OHIO
Oct'41:233

ANXIOUS SEAT
Jun'41:141

APOSTACY
Feb'32:31

APOSTLES
Jan'33:5
Feb'33:29

APOSTLES CREED
Apr'41:88

APOSTOLIC ADVOCATE
Jun'34:128
Feb'35:33
May'37C:100,117

APPLEGATE, I.
Jan'38:15

ARABIA
Dec'39:268

ARCHAEOLOGY
Oct(ieSep)'37C:174

ARKANSAS
Aug'32:192
Dec'34:282

ARMENIANISM
May'33:116

ARMSTRONG, G. (KENTUCKY)
Jan'37C:23

Arny, W. F. M.
(Article on Christian unity)
May'37C:101

ARROW ROCK, MISSOURI
Jul'40:156

ART
Feb-Mar'37C:55

ASBURY, C. (KENTUCKY)
Jan'37C:23

ASHBURN"S CREEK, TENNESSEE
Nov'40:257

Ashley, John C.
Letter. Jul'32:167
Letter. Nov'32:263

ASHTON, J. S. (INDIANA)
May'37C:120

ATHEISM
Feb'32:42
Aug'41:191

ATHENS, ALABAMA
Dec'34:282

ATWATER, D. (OHIO)
Feb'35:43

Atwater, Darwin
Letter. Nov'33:261

AUGUSTA, KENTUCKY
Mar'40:69
Jun'40:144
Jul'42:168

AURORA, OHIO
Aug'33:190
Oct'33:234
Jan'38:15
May'40:113

Austen, George (Maryland)
Letter. May'42:113

AUSTEN, GEORGE (MARYLAND)
Apr'42:75,93

AUSTIN, HIRAM
Apr'34:90

AUSTINTOWN, (TRUMBULL CO.) OHIO
Mar'39:71

Aydelotte, B. P. (Ohio)
Study of the Bible. Sep'38:201
Address. Mar'39:54

AYDELOTTE, B. P. (OHIO)
Sep'38:200
Oct'38:236

B

B., A.
Epistle from an infidel. Nov'34: 256
Observations on Dr. C. Bosworth's thoughts on the union of Christians. May'38:113
Letter. May'40:117

B., T. S. (Kentucky)
Letter. Oct(ieSep)'37C:173

BABYLON
Jan'42:18
Jul'42:149

BACHELER'S RELIGIOUS MAGAZINE
quoted. Jul'37C:148

BACON, FRANCIS
Jan'37C:19
Feb-Mar'37C:25

BACON COLLEGE
Jan'37C:12,19,21   Aug'38:184
Feb-Mar'37C:72   Sep'38:209
Apr'37C:90   Jan'39:23
May'37C:109   Mar'39:70
Jun'37C:131   Jul'39:163
Jul'37C:152   Sep'39:205,209
Aug'37C:166   May'40:102
Oct(ieSep)'37C:183 Sep'40:216
Jan'38:23   Aug'41:190
Jun'38:144   Jan'42:23

Bainbridge, Thomas
An affecting incident. Oct'41:221

BAKER, CLARISSA (KENTUCKY)
Nov'42:262

BALAAM
Jul'32:150

BALDRIDGE. (OHIO)
Jan'35:24

Baldridge, Daniel (Ohio)
Progress of Reform. Mar'34:71
Letter. May'38:117

BALDRIDGE, DANIEL (OHIO)
May'38:104

BALDRIDGE, O. (INDIANA)
Sep'33:212

Baldwin, V. V.
Progress of Reform. Feb'34:47
Letter. Jun'35:134

BALDWIN, V. V.
Jun'35:134
Aug'37C:167
Oct(ieSep)'37C:183

BALLANTINE, WILLIAM
Jun'34:122
Jul'34:153

BALTIMORE, MARYLAND
Mar'33:72   Nov'40:255
Jan'34:23   Dec'40:282
Mar'34:71   Jan'41:23
Apr'34:95   Jul'41:161
Aug'34:192   Apr'42:74
Feb'35:42   May'42:113
Dec'38:288

BANBURY, ENGLAND
Dec'42:282,283

BANKS, PRATER (INDIANA)
Sep'35:216

BANNER OF TRUTH (LEXINGTON, KY)
Jan'33:24

Banton, G. W.
Dec'33:284

BANTON'S FERRY, ?
Dec'33:284

BAPTISM
Feb'32:60   Aug'32:173
Apr'32:87   Sep'32:199
May'32:106   Sep'32:185(ie203)
Jun'32:143   Sep'32:207
Jul'32:146   (cont. next page)

5

BAPTISM (cont.)

Feb'33:46	Dec'38:283
Mar'33:49,61	May'39:114
Apr'33:78	Sep'39:193
May'33:110	Mar'40:70
Jun'33:141,142	Apr'40:96
Sep'33:193	May'40:112
Oct'33:217	Dec'40:278
Nov'33:241	Jan'41:24
Dec'33:266	Mar'41:55
Feb'34:30	May'41:106
Mar'34:57,68	Aug'41:178,181,186
Apr'34:82	Sep'41:193,215
May'34:97,110	Oct'41:227,234
Jun'34:142	Nov'41:252,262
Oct'34:238	Dec'41:275
Jan'35:17	Jan'42:9
Dec'35:269	Mary'42:102,110
Jun'37C:121,122	Jul'42:152
Apr'38:95	

BAPTIST BANNER
Sep'39:206

BAPTIST - DISCIPLE UNION
Jul'37C:139
Jun'41:127

BAPTISTS
May'33:116,117,118
Mar'34:68
Jun'34:123
Jan'35:21
Jul'37C:139
May'38:115
Aug'41:179

BARBEE, J. (KENTUCKY)
Jan'37C:23

BARKER. (NEW YORK)
Apr'42:83

BARKER, LUKE (NEW YORK)
Apr'32:95

BARNES. (ALABAMA)
Aug'40:190

BARNES. (KENTUCKY)
Oct'39:237

BARNES, JOHN (SOUTH CAROLINA)
Feb'38:48

BARNS. (OHIO)
Apr'34:91

BARNSVILLE, NEW YORK
Apr'34:94

BARR, WILLIAM V. (OHIO)
Jan'37C:22,24

BARTON, W. (MISSOURI)
May'42:118

BAUSMAN, P. N. (PENNSYLVANIA)
Jan'37C:24

BEACH WOODS, KENTUCKY
May'32:112

BEAR CREEK (BOON CO.) MISSOURI
Oct'39:238
Nov'39:263
Apr'41:95

BEASLY, ?
Jan'37C:11

BEASLEY'S CREEK, ?
Jun'32:143
Jul'32:166

BEATTY, F. (KENTUCKY)
Jan'37C:23

Becton, Fred E. (Tennessee)
Letter. Apr'32:95
Letter. Jun'32:140
Letter. Aug'32:188

BEDFORD, OHIO
May'40:113

BEDINGTON, ENGLAND
Dec'42:282

BEECHER.
Jun'32:124
Jul'32:165
Jul'33:145

BEECHER, L. (OHIO)
Aug'33:192

BEESLEY'S CREEK, KENTUCKY
Dec'41:284

BEGG. (KENTUCKY)
Oct'40:218

BEGG, W. (INDIANA)
Jun'42:142

Begg, William (Kentucky)
Letter. Sep'39:205
Letter. Jan'42:21

BEGG, WILLIAM (KENTUCKY)
Jan'39:24
May'40:101

BEHAVIOR
    See
CHRISTIAN LIFE

BELLEVIEW, KENTUCKY
Sep'42:215

BELLVILLE, INDIANA
Dec'39:284

BEN DAVIS CREEK, INDIANA
Dec'33:287

Benedict, H. T. N.
Letter. Apr'37C:92

BENEVOLENCE
Jan'38:7
Jul'40:153
Jul'42:156

BENNETT.
Mar'35:64

Bentley, Adamson
Letter. Sep'39:205
Letter. May'40:113

BENTLEY, ADAMSON
Jan'38:15
quoted. Dec'38:273
Oct'39:237

BENTON, ALABAMA
Aug'35:192

BEREAN (SPRINGFIELD, ILLINOIS)
Aug'38:186

BERRY, L. (KENTUCKY)
Jan'37C:23

BETHANY, KENTUCKY
Sep'42:215

BETHANY, VIRGINIA
Jan'33:23
Jan'38:9

BETHEL, KENTUCKY
May'32:112
Oct(ieSep)'37C:176
Sep'39:205
Sep'42:215

BETHEL, MISSOURI
Sep'33:214

BETHLEHEM (BOURBON CO.) KENTUCKY
Sep'40:213

BIBB, RICHARD
May'33:116

BIBLE
Apr'33:73
Jul'33:164,165
Oct'34:240
Sep'35:203
Aug'38:181
Dec'39:281
Jan'40:22
May'40:110
Jun'40:121
Jul'42:155

BIBLE ADVOCATE (J. R. HOWARD)
Proposal. Jun'42:143

BIBLE--CHRONOLOGY
May'42:108
Sep'42:193
Nov'42:253,254

BIBLE--COLPORTAGE
  See
 BIBLE--DISTRIBUTION

BIBLE--CRITICISM, INTERPRETATION, ETC.
May'32:117
Dec'33:266
Oct'34:236

BIBLE--DISTRIBUTION
Oct'42:240

BIBLE. N.T.
Nov'34:256,259
Dec'34:265

BIBLE. N.T. CAMPBELL
Jul'33:165

BIBLE. O.T.
Jun'33:126

BIBLE. O.T. MANUSCRIPTS
Oct'34:240

BIBLE. O.T.--VERSIONS
Aug'32:169
Sep'32:193
Dec'32:274
Jun'33:137

BIBLE READING
May'32:114
Jul'32:161

BIBLE--STUDY
Feb'32:37	Oct'33:236
Mar'32:67	Jun'38:135
Jun'32:136	Aug'38:171
Aug'32:185	Sep'38:201
Jul'33:154	Jan'39:18
Aug'33:171	May'39:107.112

BIBLE--TRANSLATIONS
   See
 BIBLE--VERSIONS

BIBLE--VERSIONS
Oct'38:218

BIBLICAL REPERTORY AND PRINCETON
         REVIEW
quoted. Mar'42:65

BIG CREEK, ILLINOIS
Jan'42:22

BIG SPRING, KENTUCKY
May'35:112

BISHOPS
Mar'40:57
Apr'40:90,96
Jun'40:133,134
Oct'40:229
Jan'42:19

BLACK, JAMES D. (KENTUCKY)
Sep'33:213

BLACKBURN, W. (KENTUCKY)
May'40:101,114

BLAIR. (NEW YORK)
Jun'42:140

Blazen, W. (Ohio)
Letter. Sep'39:208

BLEDSOE, H. M. (KENTUCKY)
Jan'37C:23

BLEDSON, HIRAM W.
Jul'40:155

BLOOMINGTON, INDIANA
Sep'33:214
Oct'41:232

Bodenhamer, W.
Letter. Oct'33:234

BOHANON, H. B. (KENTUCKY)
Jan'37C:24

BOHANON, H. C. (KENTUCKY)
Jan'37C:24

BONES
Mar'42:50

8

BOOK OF MORMON
 Jul'39:158
 Jan'41:17
 Feb'41:42
 Mar'41:62
 May'41:111

BOON, H. L. (MISSOURI)
 Apr'41:95
 May'42:118

Bootwright, William (Virginia)
 Progress of Reform. Mar'34:71

BOSTON DAILY ADVERTISER
 quoted. Jul'39:158

Bosworth, Cyrus
 Success of the Gospel. Oct(ieSep)
   '37C:177
 On union.
   Feb'38:25
   Mar'38:49
   Apr'38:88
 On forbearance. Jun'38:128
   Jul'38:145
BOSWORTH, CYRUS
 Jan'38:15
 Apr'38:89
 May'38:113

Bosworth, M. (Ohio)
 Progress of Reform. Feb'34:47

BOSWORTH, M. (OHIO)
 Jan'38:15

BOWLING GREEN, INDIANA
 May'38:117

BOWMAN, A. H. (KENTUCKY)
 Jan'37C:23

BOWMAN, JOHN (KENTUCKY)
 Jan'37C:23,24

Bowring.
 The Jews' love of Judea.
   Sep'40:211

BOYLE, J. T. (KENTUCKY)
 Jan'37C:23

BRACKEN, KENTUCKY
 Apr'32:95
 Jan'37C:11

BRADDOCK'S FIELDS, PENNSYLVANIA
 Aug'32:190

BRADFORD, C. (OHIO)
 Aug'33:192

BRADFORD, E. (KENTUCKY)
 Jan'37C:23

BRAGG, E. (ALABAMA)
 Aug'40:190

BRAGG, NEWPORT (ALABAMA)
 Aug'40:190

BRECKENRIDGE. (PRESBYTERIAN)
 Apr'33:73

BREDEN, W. W. (KENTUCKY)
 Jan'37C:23

BRIMFIELD, OHIO
 Aug'33:190

BROAD RIDGE (GRANT CO.) KENTUCKY
 May'42:115

BROADDUS, ANDREW
 May'33:118
 Aug'33:177

BROADDUS, W. F. (BAPTIST)
 Jun'41:129

Brotwright. (Virginia)
 Letter. May'32:119

BROWERING SETTLEMENT, KENTUCKY
 Jun'42:141

BROWN. (INDIANA)
 Jul'39:163

BROWN. (KENTUCKY)
 Sep'39:205
 Jun'41:140

Brown, H. - BURNET

Brown, Henry B
  Query. Oct'41:227
  Letter. Feb'42:46

BROWN, HENRY B.
  Jan'42:20

BROWN, HENRY L. (KENTUCKY)
  May'42:115

BROWN, JOHN. 1761-1835
  Obituary. Jul'35:168

Brown, Mary Ann
  Thy will be done (poem)
      Mar'42:72

BROWN, R. T. (INDIANA)
  Jul'42:160

Brown, R. T. (Ohio)
  Letter. May'38:103

BROWN, W. (KENTUCKY)
  Sep'40:214

BROWNSBOROUGH, INDIANA
  Sep(ieOct)'37C:195

BRUCE. (INDIANA)
  Jan'42:21

Bruce, R. C. (Virginia)
  Letter. May'38:117

BRUCEVILLE, INDIANA
  Jan'42:21

BRUNETSTOWN, KENTUCKY
  Jul'39:163

BRUSH. (OHIO)
  Jan'37C:24

BRYAN, B. (KENTUCKY)
  Jan'37C:23

BRYANT, J. (KENTUCKY)
  Jan'37C:23

Bryant, Joseph
  Letter. Mar'35:68

Buchanan, N. (Indiana)
  Leter. Sep(ieOct)'37C:195

BUCKLEY. (KENTUCKY)
  Jun'42:142

Buckley, W. C. (Kentucky)
  Letter. Aug'41:189

BUFORD, J. (KENTUCKY)
  Jan'37C:23

BULLARD. (VIRGINIA)
  May'42:117

BURGESS, M. R. (KENTUCKY)
  May'38:120

BURLINGTON (BOON CO.) KENTUCKY
  Jul'39:167
  Jul'42:167

BURLINGTON, OHIO
  Jul'38:167

BURNAM, H. (MISSOURI)
  Sep'33:214

Burnet, David Staats
  Letter. Oct'32:239
  Letter. Dec'33:281
  Justice. Jul'34:159
      Aug'34:174
  General meeting. Oct'35:240
  Prospectus for Christian
      Preacher. Nov'35:264
  Letter. May'37C:106
  Female Athenaeum. Oct'39:240

BURNET, DAVID STAATS
  Jun'32:142   Jan'38:22
  quoted. Jul'32:166 Jun'38:143
  Sep'34:204   Aug'38:182
  Nov'34:261   Sep'38:210
  Dec'34:282   Sep'39:205
  Jan'35:24   Aug'40:192
  Feb'35:48   Oct'41:233
  Jul'37C:151   Jun'42:143
  Oct(ieSep)'37C: Nov'42:263
      176,178,183

10

BURNS, J. (KENTUCKY)
 Jan'37C:23

BURTON. (MISSOURI)
 Apr'41:95

Burton, G. W. (Tennessee)
 Letter. Oct'32:238

Burton, J. J. (Indiana)
 Progress of Reform. Mar'34:72
 Letter. Jul'34:163
 Letter. May'38:117

BUTLER. (MRS. JAMES A.)(ALABAMA)
 Aug'40:190

Butler, Chancey
 Exclusion. Sep'35:216

BUTLER, CHAUNCY (INDIANA)
 Jun'34:144

BUTLER, HARRIET C. (ALABAMA)
 Aug'40:190

Butler, James A. (Alabama)
 Letter. Oct'32:238
 Letter. Dec'33:283
 Letter. Aug'35:191
 News. Jan'39:24
 Letter. Aug'40:190

BUTLER, JAMES A. (ALABAMA)
 quoted. Nov'34:260
 Dec'34:282
 May'37C:100,120

BUTLER, M. (KENTUCKY)
 Aug'33:192

BUTLER, NEW YORK
 Jan'35:21

11

C

C., J.
The primitive church. Feb'38:28
Universalism. Aug'39:188
The past year. Jan'40:15
Unity of the Spirit. Feb'40:36
Matthew XVII:24,27. Feb'40:37
Matthew XVIII:1. Feb'40:38
The institutes of religion.
   Feb'40:39
Luke VII (poem). Feb'40:47

C., J. jr.
Letter. May'38:118

C., M.
Obituary of Elizabeth M. Jameson.
   Jul'41:167

CADIZ, OHIO
Apr'32:95
Dec'33:283

CAESAR, JULIUS
Sep'38:197

Calahan, J. (Kentucky)
Letter. Dec'39:284

CALAHAN, J. (KENTUCKY)
Jun'37C:136

CALDWELL, WILLIAM (INDIANA)
Sep'35:216

CALERMAN. (KENTUCKY)
May'38:120

CALVINISM
May'33:116,118
Apr'37C:83
Oct'40:225

CAMBRIDGE, KENTUCKY
Jul'32:166
Oct'38:232

Campbell. (Virginia)
Letter. Sep'33:212

Campbell, Alexander
Letter. Oct'33:233
Letter. Jul'34:167
Letter. Jul'35:168
Note. Jul'39:160
Letter. Oct'39:237
Letter. Nov'39:259
Letter. Aug'40:191

CAMPBELL, ALEXANDER
May'32:119   Oct(ieSep)'37C:1
Nov'32:252   Jan'38:8,15,23
Jan'33:3   quoted. Feb'38:4
Mar'33:51   Aug'38:180
May'33:118   Dec'38:268
Jun'33:130   Mar'39:67
Dec'33:281   quoted. Oct'39:2
Jan'34:20,23   Jul'40:157
Mar'34:71   Sep'40:201
Jul'34:166   Oct'40:224
Sep'34:195,202   Nov'40:241
Dec'34:282   quoted. Jan'41:2
Mar'35:68   Jun'41:128
Nov'35:259   Feb'42:45

CAMPBELL, ALEXANDER. DEBATE WITH
      R. OWEN.
Jan'35:24

CAMPBELL, ALEXANDER. DEBATE WITH
      PURCELL
Jan'37C:18
Apr'37C:93
Jun'37C:136
Jul'37C:152

CAMPBELL, B. (ALABAMA)
Jan'37C:24

CAMPBELL, DAVID. ILLUSTRATIONS OF
      PROPHECY...
Jun'41:143
Sep'42:205

Campbell, George (Ohio)(Kentucky)
Letter. Sep'42:215

CAMPBELL, GEORGE (OHIO)(KENTUCKY)
  May'38:103
  Aug'40:187
  Oct'41:231,233

CAMPBELL, GEORGE (SCOTLAND)
  May'32:117
  Dec'32:274
  Jan'33:10

CAMPBELL, JACOB (OHIO)
  Nov'32:263

CAMPBELL, MARGARET (OHIO)
  Obituary. Nov'32:263

Campbell, Thomas
  Prospectus of religion. Jul'39:149

CAMPBELL, THOMAS
  May'32:119
  quoted. Jan'33:3
  Jan'33:17
  Dec'33:281
  Dec'34:282
  Dec'38:268
  quoted. Jun'40:127

CAMPBELLITES
    See also
  REFORMATION--19TH CENTURY
  Nov'40:259

CANADA
  Aug'33:189

CANE RIDGE, KENTUCKY
  Sep'33:214
  Apr'38:85
  May'38:118
  Dec'40:284
  Aug'41:189,190

CANE RUN ACADEMY (KENTUCKY)
  Jul'37C:151

CANE RUN, MISSOURI
  Sep'33:214

CANE SPRINGS (WOODFORD CO.) KENTUCKY
  Oct'41:233

CANFIELD, OHIO
  Jan'38:11
  May'40:120

CANNON, J. (KENTUCKY)
  Jan'37C:24

CANNON, M. (KENTUCKY)
  Jan'37C:24

CANTON, OHIO
  Oct'33:234

CARLEE. (TENNESSEE)
  Jun'32:140

CARLISLE, KENTUCKY
  Sep'33:213
  May'37C:117
  Oct'39:236

Carman. (Maryland)
  Letter. Feb'35:42

CARMAN. (MARYLAND)
  May'42:114

Carman, I. N. (Maryland)
  Letter. Mar'33:72

Carman, W. (Maryland)
  Progress of Reform. Mar'34:71

CARMAN, WILLIAM (MARYLAND)
  Dec'40:283

CAROL, JOSHUA (OHIO)
  Dec'33:284

CARROLLTON (GREEN CO.) ILLINOIS
  May'33:110
  Oct'34:239

CARTHAGE, OHIO
  Jan'33:24   Oct(ieSep)'37C:1
  Oct'33:238   Jan'38:22
  Jun'34:144   May'38:103
  Aug'35:190   Sep'38:213
  Oct'35:240   Jan'39:23,24
  May'37C:117   Apr'40:96
  Jul'37C:151   (cont. next page

CARTHAGE, OHIO (cont.)
Aug'40:192
Sep'40:216
Nov'40:263
Dec'40:276
Mar'41:72
May'41:120
Sep'41:216
Oct'41:230

CASAD, J. F. (OHIO)
Aug'35:189

CASSELLY, E. P. (OHIO)
Jan'37C:24

CAT CREEK, OHIO
Sep'32:215

CATECHISMS
Sep'32:206
Dec'32:282

CATHOLIC CHURCH
Mar'32:72   Jan'37C:18
Apr'33:73   Apr'37C:93
Oct'33:229   May'37C:113
Jan'34:10   Aug'37C:153
Jun'34:143   May'41:100
Jul'35:145   Aug'41:172
Aug'35:178,182   Sep'42:207
Sep'35:208   Oct'42:235
Dec'35:272

CATHOLIC CHURCH. POPE
Sep'33:214
Apr'37C:93
May'38:106

CAYUGA, NEW YORK
Aug'33:190

CECIL
quoted. Jan'37C:6

CEDAR DAM (FRANKLIN CO.) INDIANA
Sep'42:216

CENTRE, PENNSYLVANIA
Aug'32:190

CERINTHINAS
Nov'35:255

Challen, James
Confession. Nov'32:249
For the Evangelist. Dec'32:277
(poem) Apr'33:93
(poem) Oct'33:240
Progress of the Gospel. May'34:
117
Dear Brother. May'34:119
Lafayette Seminary. Feb'35:45
(Untitled article) Apr'37C:76
Letter. Jul'38:167
The grand national baptism of
Israel. Sep'39:193
Letter. Feb'40:41
Letter. Sep'41:216
Letter. Aug'42:188
Many of the articles signed J.C.
were probably written by
James Challen. See also
entries for C., J.

CHALLEN, JAMES
Sep'32:215   Jan'38:15
Jan'33:24   Aug'38:191
Jun'35:125   Jan'39:24
Oct'35:239   Jul'39:154
Jan'37C:23   May'40:101
Oct(ieSep)'37C: Oct'41:230,23?
176

Chambers, Uriel B.
Letter to A. Campbell. Sep'34:20?

CHAMBERS, URIEL B.
Sep'34:204

CHARITY
See
BENEVOLENCE

CHARLESTON, INDIANA
Jul'39:163

CHASE, S. P. (OHIO)
Aug'33:192

CHILDREN
May'32:118

CHILES, D. (KENTUCKY)
Jan'37C:24

CHINNOWITH'S RUN (JEFFERSON CO.)
    KENTUCKY
May'39:119

CHOCTAW ACADEMY (KENTUCKY)
    Jun'35:127

CHOLERA
    Oct'35:239

THE CHRISTIAN (EATON)
    Jun'41:142
    Jul'41:164

CHRISTIAN (JOHNSON AND SCOTT)
    Jan'37C:20
    Apr'37C:76
    Receipts. Apr'37C:96
    Terms. May'37C:97
    May'37C:101
    Receipts. May'37C:116
    Terms. Jun'37C:121
    Terms. Jul'37C:137
    Terms. Aug'37C:153
    Aug'37C:166
    Terms. Oct(ieSep)'37C:168
    Receipts. Oct(ieSep)'37C:183
    Terms. Sep(ieOct)'37C:184

CHRISTIAN AS A NAME
    Apr'35:87(ie85)
    Apr'35:87
    Oct'39:217,219,230
    Nov'39:259
    Mar'40:49,60
    May'40:115,117
    Jun'40:122,141
    Aug'40:172,179,189
    Sep'40:214,215
    Nov'40:241,242,258

CHRISTIAN BAPTIST (CAMPBELL)
    Dec'38:268
    Aug'39:190
    quoted. Feb'40:41
    Apr'42:87

CHRISTIAN BAPTIST (REVISED BY
    D. S. BURNET)
    Dec'34:288(ie284)   Feb'35:48
    Jan'35:24   Jun'35:144

CHRISTIAN CASKET
    Prospectus. Oct'33:240
    quoted. Dec'33:285

CHRISTIAN CHARACTER
    See
    CHRISTIAN LIFE

CHRISTIAN COLLEGE (NEW ALBANY, IND.)
    Sep'34:205
    Mar'35:65

CHRISTIAN-DISCIPLE UNION
    May'32:110

CHRISTIAN DISCIPLES AS A NAME
    Nov'39:258

CHRISTIAN FAMILY LIBRARY
    (CRIHFIELD)
    Prospectus. Oct'41:235
    Dec'41:284
    quoted. Feb'42:47
    quoted. Jul'42:154

CHRISTIAN FELLOWSHIP
    Jul'37C:137
    Oct(ieSep)'37C:172
    Mar'38:59
    May'38:97

CHRISTIAN GAZETTE
    quoted. Sep'35:208

CHRISTIAN HERALD AND JOURNAL
    quoted. Jul'41:147

CHRISTIAN HYMN BOOK
    Aug'39:192
    Sep'39:216
    Oct'39:239
    Dec'39:276

CHRISTIAN LIFE
    May'32:97   Jan'35:20,21
    Jun'32:126   Mar'35:61,71
    Jul'32:153   Apr'35:90
    Nov'32:245,247 Aug'35:172
    Dec'32:265   Sep'35:193
    Jan'34:40   Nov'35:244,251
    Apr'34:85   (cont. next page)

15

CHRISTIAN LIFE (cont.)
Jan'37C:3,6
Apr'37C:89
May'37C:97,111
Jan'38:6
Oct'38:220
Nov'38:241
Mar'39:62,68,69
May'39:97
Dec'39:279
Jan'40:5,6
Feb'40:25,26
Feb'40:28,39
Mar'40:49,71
Apr'40:77,82
May'40:102,104,107
Jun'40:128
Jul'40:145,148
Jul'40:153,156
Aug'40:184,185

Sep'40:193,203,205
Oct'40:225,236
Nov'40:259
Dec'40:265
Mar'41:65
May'41:115
Jun'41:130
Jul'41:152
Aug'41:191
Jan'42:7,12
May'42:100,101
May'42:102,104
Jun'42:123,124,129
Jun'42:134,136
Jul'42:148,153,160
Aug'42:173
Oct'42:233,238
Dec'42:270

CHRISTIAN MESSENGER (ENGLAND)
Aug'40:192
Oct'40:232
quoted. Nov'40:261

CHRISTIAN MESSENGER (LEXINGTON, KY)
quoted. May'32:110
Sep'34:195
Dec'34:281

CHRISTIAN MESSENGER (STONE)
Jan'40:24
Jul'41:164
May'42:102,110

CHRISTIAN PALLADIUM
Jan'41:23
Jun'41:144
quoted. Jul'41:149

CHRISTIAN PANOPLIST (KENTUCKY)
May'37C:100

CHRISTIAN PREACHER
Prospectus. Nov'35:264
quoted. Oct(ieSep)'37C:177
Jan'38:22
quoted. Aug'38:185
Jul'41:164

CHRISTIAN PUBLISHER
May'37C:99
quoted. Jun'37C:131
Aug'38:183
Feb'42:45

CHRISTIAN REFORMER (J. R. HOWARD)
Jun'37C:136

CHRISTIAN UNION
Feb'35:35
May'37C:101
Jun'37C:133
Aug'37C:153
Feb'38:25
Mar'38:49
Apr'38:88,89,90
May'38:113
Jun'38:128
Jul'38:145

Sep'38:211
Jul'39:150
Feb'40:36
Apr'40:79
Apr'41:86
May'41:119
Jun'41:127,14
Sep'41:193
Oct'42:226

CHRISTIANITY
Jan'32:3
Mar'32:49
Jun'34:130,138
Feb'35:25
Oct'35:224
Nov'35:253
Jan'38:8

Christianos
Letter. Apr'34:88

CHRONICLE OF THE CHURCH
quoted. May'40:112

CHURCH. (MISSOURI)
Sep'40:216

Church, Samuel (Pennsylvania)
Letter. Sep'35:204
A fragment. Jun'38:142
Letter. Jul'42:165
Letter. Aug'42:190

CHURCH, SAMUEL (PENNSYLVANIA)
Sep'35:205
Jan'38:9,15
quoted. Jan'41:23

Feb'42:33
Apr'42:86
Sep'42:199

CHURCH
May'32:103	Oct'35:222
Feb'33:34	Apr'39:94
Mar'33:53	May'39:98
Aug'33:169	Jul'39:150
Nov'33:259	May'40:97,99
Aug'35:186	Mar'41:61
Sep'35:214	

CHURCH AND STATE
Jul'33:162

CHURCH ATTENDENCE
Jan'40:13

CHURCH BUILDINGS
Jun'32:143
Mar'34:63
Nov'40:87

CHURCH COOPERATION
May'38:103

CHURCH DISCIPLINE
Feb'32:29	Mar'39:71,72
Mar'33:72	Jan'40:8,10
Jan'34:18	Jan'40:12,18
Mar'34:63	Feb'40:34
Apr'34:96	Apr'40:75
Jun'35:135,136	Aug'40:169
Mar'38:72	Nov'40:252
Jun'38:132	Dec'40:273,276
Sep'38:214	Apr'41:89

CHURCH, EARLY
Feb'32:31
Feb'38:28
Mar'38:60
May'38:97

CHURCH FINANCE
Sep'35:212
Jun'40:142

CHURCH GOVERNMENT
Jul'32:157	Dec'35:265,281
Jan'34:17	Apr'40:87,88
Sep'35:196	Jun'40:133,134,143
Oct'35:217	Jul'40:161
Nov'35:241	Dec'42:265

CHURCH HISTORY
Feb'32:31
Sep(ieOct)'37C:195

CHURCH MEETINGS
Mar'33:59

CHURCH MEMBERSHIP
See also
"GOOD CONFESSION"
Mar'40:56
May'42:101

CHURCH OF ENGLAND
Sep'39:201

CHURCH OF SCOTLAND
Apr'40:84

CHURCH OFFICERS
Jul'32:157
Sep'32:198
Mar'34:62,63
Jul'39:161
Mar'40:57

CHURCH ORDER
See
CHURCH GOVERNMENT

CHURCH ORGANIZATION
See
CHURCH GOVERNMENT

CHURCHING
See also
CHURCH DISCIPLINE
Feb'32:29
Sep'35:216

CILLY, JONATHAN (MAINE)
Sep'38:204

CINCINNATI, OHIO
Jul'32:165	Jan'39:24
Jan'33:24	Mar'39:72
Nov'34:261	Sep'39:208
Oct'35:240	Feb'40:41
May'37C:106	Mar'40:72
Mar'38:57	Apr'42:73

17

CIRCUMCISION
May'32:106
Jul'32:145
Jul'34:156

CIVIL ENGINEERING
Mar'35:72

CIVILIZATION
Nov'39:253
Mar'40:67

CLAPP, ALICIA
Obituary. Feb'39:48

CLAPP, M.
Jan'38:15

Clapp, Matthew S. (Ohio)
Letter. Jan'34:20

CLAPP, MATTHEW S. (OHIO)
Feb'39:48

CLARK, ELENORA (OHIO)
Obituary. Dec'39:287

CLARK, MILLIKAN (OHIO)
Dec'39:287

CLARK, WILLIAM (NORTH CAROLINA)
Mar'34:71

CLAY, HENRY
Jun'35:124

CLAYSVILLE (HARRISON CO.) KENTUCKY
Oct'41:231

CLAYSVILLE (PENNSYLVANIA OR VIRGINIA)
Jan'33:22

CLEAR CREEK (HENRY CO.) KENTUCKY
May'37C:116
Oct'40:220

CLEAR CREEK (WOODFORD CO.) KENTUCKY
Mar'32:71
Jul'32:166

CLELAND.
Sep'33:197

Clemens.
Let them alone.
Jun'35:128
Aug'35:169

CLERGY
Jan'35:22
Apr'35:93
May'35:117
Jun'35:128
Aug'35:169
Sep'35:197
Apr'37C:73
Aug'38:174,185,189
Sep'39:208
Mar'40:62
Jul'40:162
Oct'40:224,22
Nov'40:242
Jun'41:126
Jul'41:163
Aug'41:175
Oct'41:226
Nov'41:249
Apr'42:87,89

CLERGY SALARIES
Jul'35:162
Oct'35:220,233
Sep'39:209
Jun'40:142

CLINTONVILLE, KENTUCKY
Sep'38:210
Dec'38:266
Jun'41:144

Clore, Benjamine
Letter. Jun'34:139

CLOTHING AND DRESS
Jul'42:157

CLOUD, CALEB (KENTUCKY)
Jan'37C:24

CLOVERDALE, INDIANA
Oct'41:232

Cole, W. R. (Ohio)
Letter. Feb'35:43

COLEMAN. (VIRGINIA)
Aug'38:183

COLEMAN, R. S. (VIRGINIA)
May'37C:99

COLLEGE OF PROFESSIONAL TEACHERS
Aug'33:192

COLLEGES AND UNIVERSITIES
    See also names of Colleges
Jun'40:140

COLLINS. (OHIO)
Sep'39:205

COLLINS, JOSEPH
Jul'37C:152

COLLINS, W.
Jan'38:15

COLMANSVILLE, KENTUCKY
Jun'41:140

COLUMBIA, INDIANA
Dec'33:286

COLUMBIA, MISSOURI
Oct'39:238
Nov'39:263
Apr'41:95
Sep'41:214

COLVER, NATHANIEL (BAPTIST)
Dec'42:278

COMBE, GEORGE (SCOTLAND)
quoted. May'42:107

COMBS. (INDIANA)
Jun'42:142

COMBS, JOB (INDIANA)
quoted. Jan'41:23

COMBS, MICHAEL (INDIANA)
Sep'33:214
May'34:114
quoted. Jun'35:135

COMMINGSVILLE, OHIO
Sep'42:215

COMMON SCHOOL ADVOCATE (OHIO)
May'37C:100

COMMON SCHOOL ADVOCATE AND JOURNAL
    OF EDUCATION (ILLINOIS)
May'37C:101

COMMON SCHOOL ASSISTANT (J. ORVILLE
    TAYLOR)
May'37C:100

CONFESSION
Nov'32:249
Oct(ieSep)'37C:169

CONNECTICUT
Apr'32:96
Jun'34:144

CONNERSVILLE, INDIANA
Dec'33:286
May'38:103
Jul'38:167
Aug'38:190
Jul'42:160

CONSCIENCE
Jul'39:145

CONVENTION
    See
GENERAL MEETINGS

CONVENTS
Jul'35:145
Aug'35:178

CONVERSION
May'32:103
Dec'33:270
Jun'40:135
Jul'40:150
Sep'40:195,206,208
Dec'40:267,285
Feb'41:33
Nov'41:260

COONS, JACOB (MISSOURI)
Nov'39:263

COONS, JOSEPH (MISSOURI)
Nov'39:263

COONS, S. (KENTUCKY)
Jan'37C:24

Coons, Z. (Kentucky)
Letter. Sep'39:207

19

COOPER'S RUN, KENTUCKY
Sep'38:210
May'41:120
Jun'41:140
May'42:117

Cope, J. (Indiana)
News. Jan'39:23

CORINTH, KENTUCKY
Jun'42:140
Aug'42:189

CORWIN, DANIEL
Jan'37C:18

COURT CASES (LAW)
Jan'35:21

COVENANTS
Aug'39:169

COVE'S SPRING, KENTUCKY
Sep'39:205

COVINGTON, KENTUCKY
Sep'32:215

COWDERY, OLIVER (MORMON)
Oct'38:226

Cowper, William (Poet)
Right improvement of life (poem)
Feb'42:48

CRAB ORCHARD, KENTUCKY
Oct'41:231

Craft, John B. (Indiana)
Progress of Reform. Feb'34:48

CRAIG, (MRS. HARRISON) (KENTUCKY)
Death. Jun'38:143

CRAIG. (TENNESSEE)
Jun'32:141

CRAIG, HARRISON (KENTUCKY)
Jun'38:143

CRAWFORD. (KENTUCKY)
Oct'40:220

Crawford, W.
Question. Apr'40:96

Crawford, William
Interesting. Dec'40:285
Letter. Sep'41:215

Creath, Jacob, 1777-1854
Letter. Mar'32:71

CREATH, JACOB, 1777-1854
Feb'32:30
Jul'32:166
Jan'33:24
Oct'35:239
May'37C:117
Jun'38:144
Oct'41:231

Creath, Jacob, 1799-1886
Letter. Aug'35:189
Letter. Jul'41:166

CREATH, JACOB, 1799-1886
Oct'35:239
Jul'37C:151
Oct(ieSep)'37C:176
Jun'38:144
Sep'40:216
Sep'41:214

CREEDS
May'33:118
Jan'34:9

CRENSHAW, J. (KENTUCKY)
Jan'37C:23,24

CRENSHAW, W. (KENTUCKY)
Jan'37C:24

CRIHFIELD. (KENTUCKY)
Feb'42:45

Crihfield, Arthur
The Heretic Detector and Reforme
Jul'37C:146
Letter. Oct'38:227
Conversions. Oct'38:232

CRIHFIELD, ARTHUR
May'37C:100
Mar'38:inside back cover
Oct'38:228
May'41:120
Oct'41:230,235
Dec'41:284

Crispus
Criticism. Sep'32:185(ie203)
Note. Sep'32:210

CRIST, G. T. (OHIO)
Sep'32:215

CRITTENDEN, J. J. (KENTUCKY)
Apr'42:73

CROOKED CREEK (MONROE CO.) MISSOURI
Nov'39:263

CROOKSHANK. (DR.) (PRESBYTERIAN)
Jun'34:141

THE CROSS
Jul'40:163

CROSS AND BAPTIST JOURNAL
Jul'34:159,160
Sep'34:202

Cullen, William
Calvinism. Jun'38:139

CULP'S MILLS (PENDLETON CO.)
    KENTUCKY
Jun'42:141

Cummings, A. G. (Massachusetts)
To friends of primitive Chris-
    tianity. Nov'40:263

CUMMINGS, A. G. (MASSACHUSETTS)
Nov'40:255

CUMMINSVILLE, OHIO
Jan'35:24
Aug'35:189

CURD, JOHN (KENTUCKY)
Jan'37C:23

CURSES
Jul'38:164

CUYHOGA, OHIO
Oct'39:237

CYNTHIANA, KENTUCKY
Apr'40:95
May'40:114,117
Aug'40:191
Sep'40:213
Oct'40:221
Jun'41:140

CYPRIAN
May'33:97

Cyrus, H. A. (Illinois)
Letter. Oct'34:239

D

DAMNATION
Sep'33:216

Daniel, W. (Ohio)
Letter. Jun'32:143

DANVERS, MASSACHUSETTS
May'33:116

DANVILLE, INDIANA
Dec'33:286
Jan'39:23

DANVILLE, KENTUCKY
Sep'40:216

DARK'S PRAIRIE (RANDOLPH CO.)
     MISSOURI
Nov'39:264

Darling, Smith (New York)
Letter to Mrs. Prudence Phelps.
     Oct'42:238

DARLING, SMITH (NEW YORK)
Oct'42:237

DAVENPORT, W. (ILLINOIS)
Jul'37C:151

DAVENPORT, IOWA
Mar'41:71

DAVID'S FORK, KENTUCKY
Jan'38:24

DAVIDSON, MATILDA
quoted. Jul'39:158

DAVIESS, D. (MISSOURI)
Nov'39:263

DAVIESS, J. H. (KENTUCKY)
Jan'37C:23

DAVIESS, T. (KENTUCKY)
Jan'37C:24

Davis, Jewel (Ohio)
Letter. Jun'32:142

DAVIS, WILLIAM (MISSISSIPPI)
Jan'37C:24

DAWSON. (PENNSYLVANIA)
Aug'32:190

Dawson, Jane (Pennsylvania)
Letter. Mar'32:71
Letter. Aug'32:189

Dawson, John
Discourse by S. W. Lynd.
     Apr'38:94

DAWSON, JNO. D. (KENTUCKY)
Sep(ieOct)'37C:199

DAYTON, OHIO
Apr'34:94
Jun'34:144
Jan'35:21,24
Jul'35:167
Aug'35:190
Oct'35:240
Apr'41:96
Aug'42:190
Dec'42:284

Dean, Rhoda
Death of father (Hayden).
     May'40:119

DEARFIELD, OHIO
Oct'39:237

DEATH
May'34:119
Jan'35:14
Mar'38:68
May'38:105
Nov'39:255
Oct(ieSep)'37C:171

DEATH OF CHRIST
     See
     JESUS CHRIST--DEATH AND RESURREC

Deaver, Henry J.
Letter. Sep'32:213

DEBATES
  Apr'33:73   Dec'39:284
  Jan'35:24   Jan'41:23
  Jan'37C:18   Sep'41:215
  Apr'37C:93
  Oct(ieSep)'37C:168

DELAVAN, E. C.
  Sep'38:209

DELAWARE
  Jun'32:144

DEMONOLOGY
  Feb'42:45

DENOMINATIONS
  Mar'32:72
  Apr'32:96
  Jun'32:144
  Aug'32:192
  Apr'33:90
  Jun'40:140

DEPRAVITY
    See
  SIN

DESPAIN. (KENTUCKY)
  May'40:101

DEVIL
  May'33:103
  Jan'39:23
  Nov'41:247
  Dec'41:267

DEWHIT, WILLIAM (KENTUCKY)
  Sep(ieOct)'37C:199

DIBBLE. (OHIO)
  Apr'33:95

DIBBLE, CHARLES
  Obituary. May'41:120

Dibble, Ira (Ohio)
  Letter. May'40:113

Dibble, P. K.
  Obituary of Charles Dibble.
    May'41:120

Dick, Thomas
  Contemplation of the starry
      heavens. Mar'42:61

DISASTERS
    See
  STEAMBOATS--ACCIDENTS

THE DISCIPLE   (ALABAMA)
  May'37C:100

DISCIPLES - BAPTIST UNION
    See
  BAPTIST - DISCIPLES UNION

DISCIPLE - CHRISTIAN UNION
  May'32:110

DISCIPLES OF CHRIST AS A NAME
  Oct'39:217,219,230
  Nov'39:260
  Mar'40:60
  Aug'40:172,189
  Sep'40:215
  Nov'40:258

Discipulus (Robert Richardson)
  For the Evangelist.
      no. 1. Sep'32:184(ie202)
      no. 2. Sep'32:204
      no. 3. Sep'32:211
  Baptism and remission. Oct'41:234

DISEASE
    See
  PATHOLOGY

DISTRIBUTION OF THE BIBLE
    See
  BIBLE--DISTRIBUTION

DISTRICT OF COLUMBIA
    See
  WASHINGTON, D.C.

DIXON, JACOB (METHODIST)
  Aug'34:177

DOANE. (BISHOP)
  quoted. Jul'42:156

DODGE, ROBERT P. (D.C.)
Jan'37C:22,24

Donogh, R. P. (Ohio)
Letter. Mar'39:72

Dorsey. (Pennsylvania)
Letter. Jan'33:22

DOUGLASS. (MISSOURI)
Nov'39:263

DOVER, KENTUCKY
Mar'40:69
Dec'41:284
Jul'42:168

DOVER (RANDOLPH CO.) MISSOURI
Nov'39:264
Jul'40:154

DOVER REGULAR BAPTIST ASSOCIATION
(VIRGINIA)
Aug'33:177

Dowling, Jackson (Ohio)
Progress of the Gospel. May'34:114

Dowling, William (Ohio)
Letter. Apr'33:95
Letter. Feb'35:42

DOWNING, G. (KENTUCKY)
Jan'37C:24

DRAKE, D. (OHIO)
Aug'33:192

Dratt, John (New York)
Query. Dec'35:265

DRATT, JOHN (NEW YORK)
Jan'35:21

DRESS
See
CLOTHING AND DRESS

DRIPPING SPRINGS, TENNESSEE
Sep'42:215

DRY CREEK, KENTUCKY
Oct'41:232

DRY RUN, KENTUCKY
Sep'40:213

DUELS
Sep'38:204

DUNCAN, JOHN (KENTUCKY)
Jan'37C:23

DUNGAN, FRANCIS (MARYLAND)
Apr'42:75,93

DUNKESON, WASHINGTON (KENTUCKY)
Sep'33:214

Dunn, J. H. (Tennessee)
Letter. Feb'42:47

Dunning. (Georgia)
Letter. Jun'32:143

Dunning, S. C. (Georgia)
Letter. Apr'33:94
Letter. Jun'40:142
Letter. Jul'41:166

DUTCH FORK, PENNSYLVANIA
Jan'33:22
Sep'33:212

Duval, J. (Virginia)
Letter. Jun'33:139

DUVAL, J. (VIRGINIA)
Aug'33:177

E

E., D.
  Christian order.
    Aug'35:186
    no. 2. Oct'35:217
    no. 3. Nov'35:241

E., F. W.
    See
  Emmons, F. W.

E., S. A. (Sister) (Ohio)
  Letter. Feb'35:43

EAGLE CREEK, OHIO
  Jun'42:141

EARTH
  Jan'38:3
  Feb'38:33,44
  Apr'38:73,96
  Aug'38:174
  Jun'40:131

Eaton, W. W. (New Brunswick)
  Baptism. Dec'40:278

EATON, W. W.
  Jun'41:142
  Oct'41:233

Edax
  Letter. Aug'40:189

EDUCATION
    See also
  SELF CULTURE
  Jun'33:123   Jun'38:121,133
  Feb-Mar'37C:25   Aug'38:172
  Jan'38:1,16   Sep'38:193,201,211
  Feb'38:29,36,48   Jan'39:20
  Mar'38:55   Mar'39:52,72
  Apr'38:79   May'39:100,103,106

EGYPT
  Nov'35:255

ELBA, NEW YORK
  Sep'32:215

ELDERS
  Apr'32:95
  Mar'40:58
  Jan'42:19
  Feb'42:40
  Apr'42:89

ELECTION (DOCTRINE)
  Apr'33:85

ELIZABETHTOWN, KENTUCKY
  Jan'35:22

ELIZAVILLE, KENTUCKY
  May'32:112
  May'38:120

ELK FORK (MONROE CO.) MISSOURI
  Nov'39:263

ELKHORN, KENTUCKY
  Sep'40:213
  Oct'40:220

ELKTON, KENTUCKY
  Sep'42:215

ELLEY. (KENTUCKY)
  Sep'39:206
  May'40:101
  Jan'42:24
  Jun'42:140

Elley, George W.
  Letter. Feb'32:30
  Letter' Jul'32:166

ELLEY, GEORGE W.
  Dec'40:282   Sep'42:215
  Oct'41:232,233

ELLIS. (KENTUCKY)
  Sep'32:215
  Mar'40:72

ELLIS, H. (KENTUCKY)
  Jan'37C:24

25

ELLIS, JOHN (KENTUCKY)
Oct'41:232

Ellis, John A. (Kentucky)
Letter. Sep'40:216

Ellis, John G. (Kentucky)
Letter. Sep'(ieOct)'37C:199
Letter. Jul'39:161
Letter. Sep'39:207
Letter. Apr'41:96
Letter. Sep'42:216

EMIGRATION
See
IMMIGRATION AND EMIGRATION

EMISON, JAMES (KENTUCKY)
Jan'37C:24

EMISON, WILLIAM (KENTUCKY)
Jan'37C:24

EMMERSON, JOHN (TENNESSEE)
Nov'40:257

Emmons, Francis W.
Review of "The Union of Christians"
Feb'35:35
Mar'35:53
Letter. Mar'35:70
Discourse on the Fellowship of
the First Christian congregation.
Mar'38:60
May'38:97
Letter. Dec'40:282

EMMONS, FRANCIS W.
Jan'38:22
Aug'38:180
Jul'42:160

EMMONS, FRANCIS W. THE VOICE
Jul'38:168

EMORY, JOHN (METHODIST)
Jun'38:137

Encell, John (Virginia)
Progress of Reform. Mar'34:71

ENGLAND. (BISHOP) (CATHOLIC)
Sep'33:215

ENGLAND
Sep(ieOct)'37C:194
Jul'38:160
Jan'40:20
Jul'41:158
Dec'42:282,283

ENGLES, WILLIAM M. (PRESBYTERIAN)
Mar'42:53

ENGLISH LANGUAGE
Mar'39:54

ENSEL, CHARLES (VIRGINIA)
Jan'33:23

EPHESUS
Apr'40:94

EPISCOPAL RECORDER
Nov'34:261

EPISCOPALIANS
Mar'32:72
Nov'34:261
Jan'35:17

ERRETT, HENRY (NEW YORK)
Jul'38:160

ERRETT, HENRY. AN ESSAY ON THE
ORDER AND DISCIPLINE OF THE
APOSTOLIC CHURCHES
Sep'38:214,215

Errett, Isaac
Letter. Sep'38:214

Errett, R.
Letter. Sep'38:214

ESSENES
Nov'35:254

ETERNAL LIFE
See
FUTURE LIFE

ETHICS
Aug'32:184

EUCLID, OHIO
Sep'39:205

EUROPE
Aug'42:171

EUROPE--ECONOMIC CONDITIONS
Apr'33:96

"Eusebius" (Isaac Errett)
The letter men and allegorists.
    Jul'35:153

Evangelicus
On committing the oracles.
        no. 1. Jul'33:154
        no. 2. Aug'33:171

EVANGELISM
Oct'32:218
Nov'32:241
Jan'34:1
Jan'39:5
Mar'41:69
Aug'41:180

THE EVANGELIST (WALTER SCOTT)
Jan'32:17
Jan'33:24
Oct'33:234,240
Sep'34:195,212
May'35:118
Jun'35:144
Jan'37C:20
Mar'38:back cover (inside)
Receipts. Mar'38:back cover
May'38:115
May'38:back cover
Jul'38:168
Receipts. Jul'38:back cover
Receipts. Sep'38:back cover
Oct'38:238
Receipts. May'39:120
Receipts. Jul'39:168
Receipts. Sep'39:216
Oct'39:240
Nov'39:264

THE EVANGELIST (cont.)
'40:3
Receipts. Feb'40:48
Mar'40:72
Jun'40:140
Jul'40:157
Sep'40:201
Nov'40:264
Feb'41:48
Jul'41:164
Oct'41:239
Apr'42:94
Oct'42:240

EVANGELISTS
    See
CLERGY

Evans, James
Letter. Mar'39:58

Everett, Howard (Missouri)
Progress of the Gospel. Sep'34:
    216

EWING, ALBERT
Jul'34:166

EWING, JANE CAMPBELL
Obituary. Jul'34:166

EXCLUSION FROM CHURCHES
    See
CHURCH DISCIPLINE
CHURCHING

EXTREMISM
Feb'34:34
Mar'34:49

F

F., B. (Indiana)
 Letter. Sep'39:208

FAIRFIELD, OHIO
 Jul'35:167
 Aug'35:189

FAIRVIEW, VIRGINIA
 Jan'35:24

FAITH
Mar'32:50	Spe'33:206
Apr'32:83	Oct'33:237
Jul'32:164	Apr'34:88,89
Sep'32:211	Feb'35:29
Mar'33:56	Jan'37C:6
Apr'33:82	Dec'40:275
May'33:102	Oct'41:222
Jul'33:168	Dec'42:273
Aug'33:178,182	

FALL, JAMES (KENTUCKY)
 Jan'37C:24

Fall, Philip Slater
 Letter. Sep'32:213
 Female education. Sep'38:212
 Discourse. Oct'42:226

FALL, PHILIP SLATER
 Jan'37C:14,23
 Aug'40:192
 Oct'40:221
 quoted. Oct'42:217

FAMILY
Feb'32:35	Apr'38:77
Jun'33:121	Oct'38:223
Jul'33:149	Mar'39:58
Sep'33:202	Apr'40:89
Feb'38:29	May'40:115

FAMILY TESTAMENT
    See
 BIBLE. N.T. CAMPBELL

FANNING, TOLBERT
 Apr'32:95
 Jan'37C:23

FANNIR. (TENNESSEE)
 Jun'32:140

FAR, SIMEON (INDIANA)
 Sep(ieOct)'37C:195

FARGUHARSER. (MARYLAND)
 Jan'34:22

FARIS, JAMES (KENTUCKY)
 Jan'37C:11

FARNSWORTH. (KENTUCKY)
 Jan'37C:13

Farquhar. (Ohio)
 Letter. Apr'32:95

FARQUHARSON, CHARLES (MARYLAND)
 Nov'40:255
 Oct'41:232

FAVER, JOHN, SR. (ALABAMA)
 Dec'34:282

FAYETTE (HOWARD CO.) MISSOURI
 Oct'39:238
 Nov'39:263
 Apr'41:95
 Jul'41:165

FEET WASHING
    See
 FOOT WASHING

FELICITY (CLERMONT CO.) OHIO
 Oct'35:240

FELLOWSHIP
    See
 CHRISTIAN FELLOWSHIP

FELTER, JAMES (OHIO)
 Obituary. Dec'41:283

FEMALE ATHENAEUM
 Aug'40:192

FEMALE COLLEGIATE INSTITUTE
(GEORGETOWN, KENTUCKY)
Jan'37C:16   Sep'39:205
Jan'38:title page Apr'40:96
Mar'38:back cover Jun'40:138
May'38:120   Sep'40:206
Oct'38:233   Aug'42:186
May'39:106   Nov'42:262

FEMALE INDUCTIVE ACADEMY (KENTUCKY)
Jun'35:134

FEMALE SEMINARY (WOODFORD CO.,
KENTUCKY)
Sep(ieOct)'37C:199

FERIS, FRANCIS
May'33:116

Feris, M. A.
(Untitled article). May'37C:105

FERN CREEK, KENTUCKY
Jan'37C:21

FERRIS. (MISSOURI)
Jul'40:154

FERRIS, M. A. (MISSOURI)
May'42:118

Field, Nathaniel
Letter. Oct'34:233
On slavery. Jan'35:17
Letter. Apr'35:77
Letter. Jun'35:138

FIELD, NATHANIEL
Feb'35:39
Jun'35:136,141
May'40:101
Jun'40:144
Aug'41:192

Fillmore, A. N.
The crisis. Dec'35:272

FINANCE
See
CHURCH FINANCE

FINLAY. (KENTUCKY)
Feb'42:45

FINLEY, JOHN (MARYLAND)
Aug'34:192
Jan'38:24

FINNELL, JOHN W. (KENTUCKY)
Jan'37C:24

FISHBACK, JAMES
Dec'35:269
Mar'40:66
Jun'41:128

FISHBACK, JAMES. PHILOSOPHY....
quoted. Jul'33:168

FLAG SPRING (CAMPBELL CO.) KENTUCKY
Mar'40:69

FLAT ROCK, INDIANA
Aug'38:190

FLAT ROCK, KENTUCKY
Apr'34:93
Sep'39:206

FLATTWOOD, KENTUCKY
Oct(ieSep)'37C:176

FLEMING. (KENTUCKY)
Sep'33:213
Oct'35:239
Sep'39:205

FLEMING, L. (KENTUCKY)
May'40:101

FLEMING, L. J.
Sep'33:212
Jun'38:144
Sep'40:214

FLEMINGSBURG, KENTUCKY
May'32:112
Oct'39:236

29

FLINN. (MISSOURI)
Jan'33:22

FLINN, L. (MISSOURI)
Sep'33:213

FLORENCE, KENTUCKY
Jul'42:167

FLORIDA (MONROE CO.) MISSOURI
Nov'39:263
Sep'41:214

FLOURNOY, T. C. (KENTUCKY)
Jan'37C:23

FLOWERS, U. G. (MISSISSIPPI)
Jan'37C:24

FOOT WASHING
May'34:119
Jan'39:24

FOREKNOWLEDGE
See
PROPHECIES

Forrard, A. (Kentucky)
Letter. Apr'32:95

Forrester, Robert (Pennsylvania)
Letter. Apr'34:94

FORRESTER, ROBERT (PENNSYLVANIA)
Mar'35:68
Jan'38:15

FORWARD. (PENNSYLVANIA)
Sep(ieOct)'37C:193

FOSTER. (SISTER) (KENTUCKY)
Jul'37C:152

FOSTER, CHARLES (OHIO)
Oct'41:237

FOSTER, JOHN (TENNESSEE)
Aug'35:191

FOUNTAINHEAD, KENTUCKY
Sep'42:215

FOURTH OF JULY
Sep'38:207

FRANCE
Jul'41:159

FRANKFORT, KENTUCKY
Sep'32:214
Oct'40:221

FRANKLIN, KENTUCKY
Sep'42:215

FRAZEE, I. J. (KENTUCKY)
Jan'37C:24

FREDRICKSBURG, VIRGINIA
May'38:117

FREEDOM (HOWARD CO.) MISSOURI
Nov'39:263

FREEMASONS
Aug'38:182

French, C.
A calculation. Jul'41:145

FRENCH, JOHN C. (MARYLAND)
Aug'34:192
Nov'40:255

A Friend of Order
Christian discipline. Jan'40:18

FRIENDSHIP (BOON CO.) MISSOURI
Oct'39:238
Nov'39:263

FRISBIE, F. G. (OHIO)
Aug'34:192

FULTON (CALLOWAY CO.) MISSOURI
Nov'39:263
Apr'41:95

FUNERALS
Nov'39:256

FUTURE LIFE
Mar'32:52   Feb'38:44
Mar'35:57   Feb'39:25
May'35:119   Mar'39:61

G

GAINES, T. N. (MISSOURI)
Jul'40:154

GALLATIN, KENTUCKY
Sep'42:215

GANO. (KENTUCKY)
Sep'33:213
Feb'38:48
Aug'38:192
Sep'39:205
Aug'40:191
Nov'40:258
Jan'41:23
Mar'41:70
May'42:115

Gano, Daniel
Letter. Jul'33:163

GANO, DANIEL
Nov'33:263
Jan'37C:18

Gano, John Allen
Great meeting in Kentucky.
    Sep'38:210
Conversions. Oct'38:232
News. Jan'39:23
Pure speech. Mar'39:66
Letter. Sep'40:213
Letter. Dec'40:284
Letter. May'41:119
Note. Dec'41:286
Progress of Reform. May'42:117

GANO, JOHN ALLEN
Apr'38:87   Mar'39:70
May'38:120   May'40:114
Jun'38:144   Oct'40:218
Jul'38:168   Jun'41:140,144
Sep'38:210   Jan'42:21
Dec'38:266   Oct'42:239

GARDNER, M.
Jan'41:23

GARDNER, MATTHEW. LEGION
Nov'35:257

GARRETTSVILLE, OHIO
Apr'34:91

GASTON, JOSEPH (OHIO)
Obituary. Feb'35:46,47
Apr'35:87(ie85)

GATES. (KENTUCKY)
Jan'34:23
Feb'34:47
May'39:119

GATES, NEW YORK
Sep'32:215

GENERAL MEETINGS
Aug'34:181

GENIUS
    See also
TALENT
May'35:107

GENIUS OF CHRISTIANITY (SALEM,
    MASSACHUSETTS)
Nov'40:256,263
Jul'41:164

GEOLOGY
Aug'40:188

GEORGE. (BAPTIST) (VIRGINIA)
May'33:118

GEORGETOWN COLLEGE (KENTUCKY)
Mar'35:72
May'35:113

GEORGETOWN, KENTUCKY
Mar'32:71   Jun'41:140
Jul'32:166   Feb'42:45
May'35:111   Oct'42:239
Jun'37C:135
Jul'37C:151
Jan'38:24
Apr'38:87
May'38:118
Sep'40:213
Oct'40:217

GEORGETOWN (PETTIS CO.) MISSOURI
Jul'40:154

GEORGETOWN (BROWN CO.) OHIO
Jan'35:23
Jan'37C:11

GEORGIA
Jun'32:143,144
Dec'34:282
Jul'41:166

GERMANTOWN, KENTUCKY
Apr'37C:96
Jun'37C:136
Mar'40:69
Dec'41:284

GERMANY
Jul'41:158

GHENT (CARROL CO.) KENTUCKY
Jun'42:141

GIBSON, W. S. (MISSISSIPPI)
Jan'37C:24

GIVEN, KENTUCKY
Sep'39:205,209
Sep'40:216

GLASGOW, KENTUCKY
May'37C:106
Jun'37C:135,136
Dec'39:284

Glaspell, James (Iowa)
Letter. Mar'41:71

Glen, Nat. E. (Virginia)
Letter. Apr'32:95

GNOSTICISM
Jun'33:134
Nov'35:255

GOD
Oct'32:222,233   Mar'39:66
Nov'32:259   May'40:108,109
Apr'34:73   Jun'40:132
Aug'37C:167   Sep'40:195,206

GODDARD, G. (KENTUCKY)
Jan'37C:24

GODDARD, W. (KENTUCKY)
Jan'37C:24

GOOD CONFESSION
May'38:119

GOODRICH, T.
Feb'41:47

GOODWIN. (INDIANA)
Oct'41:232

Goodwin, Elijah
(Untitled article). Sep(ieOct)
'37C:190

GORDON. (OHIO)
Dec'42:284

Gordon, D. (Kentucky)
Letter. Jan'34:24
Progress of Reform. Feb'34:46

GORDON, DAVID
Aug'42:190

Gordon, J. W. (Indiana)
Letter. Mar'39:71
question. May'42:120

Gosney.
Letter. Sep'32:213
Letter. Jul'35:167

Gosney, F. (Ohio)
Apr'34:94

GOSPEL
Jan'32:13
Feb'32:34
Jun'33:144
Sep'35:196
Dec'38:265
Jun'41:121

GOSPEL ADVOCATE (GEORGETOWN, KY)
Prospectus. Nov'34:264
Dec'34:281
Feb'35:45
quoted. Jul'35:163,164
Jan'37C:20

GOSPEL ADVOCATE (LEESBURGH, OHIO)
Dec'41:285

GOVERNORS
Sep'32:216
Nov'32:264

GRACE (THEOLOGY)
Aug'41:192

Grafton, Samuel
Progress of Reform. Feb'34:48
Letter. Jan'35:24
Letter. Jul'39:161
Letter. Dec'39:282

GRAFTON, SARAH S.
Dec'39:283

Graham.
(poem). Apr'33:90

GRAHAM, A. (ALABAMA)
Aug'35:191

GRAHAM, A. (KENTUCKY)
Jan'37C:24

GRAHAM, ALEXANDER (ILLINOIS)
Aug'38:186

GRANT, ASHBEL. THE NESTORIANS...
Mar'42:65

GRANT, G. (KENTUCKY)
Jan'37C:24

GRASSDALE, KENTUCKY
Sep'42:215

GRASSY SPRING (WOODFORD CO.) KENTUCKY
Oct'38:233
Oct'41:233

GRASSY SPRINGS (HENRY CO.) KENTUCKY
Oct'40:220
May'42:116

GRAVES, J. T. (KENTUCKY)
Jan'37C:24

GRAVES, J. W. (CONGRESSMAN) (KY)
Sep'38:204

GREEN, A. B. (OHIO)
Jan'38:15

GREEN, W. (KENTUCKY)
Jan'37C:24

GREENCASTLE, INDIANA
May'34:114
Jul'34:164

GREENE. (OHIO)
Jul'41:166

GREENSBURG, INDIANA
Dec'33:287

GREENVILLE INSTITUTE (HARRODSBURG,
    KENTUCKY)
Jan'42:23

Greenwell, George (England)
Letter. Dec'42:282

GRIDLEY. (PRESBYTERIAN)
Mar'34:56

GRIFFITH, J. (KENTUCKY)
Jan'37C:24

GRIFFITH'S, KENTUCKY
May'42:115

GRIGSBY. (KENTUCKY)
May'38:109

GRIGSBY, B. B. (KENTUCKY)
Sep'38:back cover

GRIMKE, THOMAS S. ADDRESS ON
THE EXPEDIENCY AND DUTY
OF ADOPTING THE BIBLE AS
A CLASS BOOK....
Review. Feb'32:37
Mar'32:67
Jun'32:136
Aug'32:185

GUANLAITES
Nov.35:254

GUIZOTT.
Nov'39:253

GUTHRIE, W. (VIRGINIA)
Jan'37C:24

H

H., J. R.
The power of God's word. Jun'38:
126

H., P.
Reformation. Nov'35:251

HADEN, JOEL H. (MISSOURI)
Sep'33:214
Nov'39:264
May'42:118

HADEN, S. (PENNSYLVANIA)
Mar'35:68

HAGGIN, J. (KENTUCKY)
Jan'37C:24

HALE, MATTHEW
quoted. Mar'33:60

HALL. (KENTUCKY)
Oct'35:239
Aug'38:182

HALL. (TENNESSEE)
Jun'32:141

Hall, Benjamin F.
The new birth. Jun'37C:122
Letter. May'40:112
A discourse on spiritual influence.
Sep'40:195
Spiritual influence. Dec'40:267

HALL, BENJAMIN F.
Nov'34:264   Mar'40:65
Dec'34:282   Mar'40:72
Feb'35:45   May'40:101,114
May'35:113   Sep'40:194,206
Oct(ieSep)'37C: Oct'40:219
  176   Oct'41:223
Jun'38:144   Jan'42:23
Jul'39:164   Jun'42:139
Oct'39:236

HALL, BENJAMIN F.   THREE SALVATIONS
Aug'38:184

HALL, LEVI N. (INDIANA)
May'38:104

HALL, ROBERT (BAPTIST)
Jun'40:138
Aug'41:177

HAMILTON. (MRS. ALEXANDER)
Jan'38:8

Hammel, Charles (Indiana)
Letter. May'39:119

HANGING FORK, KENTUCKY
Sep'39:205

HANNAH'S CREEK, INDIANA
Dec'33:286

HANOVER MEETING HOUSE, KENTUCKY
Sep(ieOct)'37C:199

HAPPINESS
Dec'39:279

HARDIN, C. (ILLINOIS)
Jan'37C:24

HARDIN, L. (OHIO)
May'37C:100

HARGRAVE, J. (OHIO)
Jan'37C:24

HARNEY, G. T. (KENTUCKY)
Apr'38:85

HARNEY, JOHN (KENTUCKY)
Feb'41:48

Harris. (Tennessee)
Letter. Mar'33:72

Harris, J. M. (Indiana)
Letter. Sep(ieOct)'37C:195

HARRIS, JOHN (ENGLAND)
Jul'38:162

Harris, John M. (Indiana)
Letter. Jun'35:144

HARRIS, MARTIN
Oct'38:226

35

HARRIS, P. - HAYDEN, C.

HARRIS, P. (INDIANA)
Oct'41:232

Harris, William
Question. May'42:120

HARRIS, WILLIAM (KENTUCKY)
Feb'40:47

HARRISON, JOHN (INDIANA)
Jan'42:21

HARRISON, INDIANA
See
HARRISON (HAMILTON CO.) OHIO

HARRISON (HAMILTON CO.) OHIO
Mar'34:71
Jun'34:140,144
Aug'34:192
Jan'35:24
Jul'37C:151
May'38:103
Jul'38:167
Apr'40:75

HARROD'S CREEK (OLDHAM CO.) KENTUCKY
Aug'39:191
Sep'39:206
Dec'42:283

HARRODSBURG, KENTUCKY
Jul'38:168
Aug'38:192
Sep'39:209
Apr'40:96
May'40:100,114
Jul'40:146
Jun'41:140
Jan'42:23
Jun'42:140

HARTSELL, I. (OHIO)
Jan'38:15

HARVEY. (OHIO)
Jan'33:24

HASTINGS, E. (KENTUCKY)
Jan'37C:24

HASTINGS, S. (KENTUCKY)
Jan'37C:24

HATCH, S. (KENTUCKY)
Jan'37C:23,24

HATCH, SAMUEL (KENTUCKY)
Sep'39:205
Jul'40:148

HATCH, WILLIAM (KENTUCKY)
Apr'38:85
Jun'38:144

HATFIELD, JONATHAN (NEW YORK)
Jul'38:160

Hathaway, D. H. (Kentucky)
Success of the Gospel. Jan'37C:
21

HAVEN, GEORGETTA (KENTUCKY)
Nov'42:262

HAWKINS, W. H.
Jun'37C:131

Hayden. (Ohio)
Letter. Jul'32:167
Letter. Sep'32:214

HAYDEN. (AMOS SUTTON'S FATHER)
Death. May'40:118
Obituary. May'40:119

HAYDEN. (PENNSYLVANIA)
Aug'32:190

HAYDEN, AMOS SUTTON
May'40:118

Hayden, Arthur (Ohio)
Progress of Reform. Feb'34:47

HAYDEN, ARTHUR
May'40:119

HAYDEN, CHRISTOPHER
May'40:119

Hayden, Daniel (Ohio)
Letter. Feb'32:47
Letter. Apr'34:93

HAYDEN, DANIEL
May'40:119

HAYDEN, SAMUEL
May'40:119

Hayden, William (Ohio)
Letter. Aug'33:190
Letter. Feb'35:44
Letter. Aug'35:192
Letter. Jul'39:161

HAYDEN, WILLIAM (OHIO)
Jan'32:24
Oct'32:239
Jun'34:144
Jan'38:15
Sep'39:205
May'40:118
Jul'41:166
Dec'42:276

HAYNES. (BAPTIST) (INDIANA)
Dec'39:284

Haywood. (Indiana)
Letter. Sep'33:212

HEALTH
    See
HYGIENE

HEAVEN
Aug'34:182   Jul'42:166
Dec'34:271
Mar'38:52
Aug'41:177
Oct'41:233

Heber, Reginald
Hymn. Mar'35:71

HEBREW LITERATURE
Jun'33:126

HEDDINGS, ELIJAH (METHODIST)
Jun'38:137

HEIDELBERGE, GEORGE F. (KENTUCKY)
Nov'42:262

HELMS. (KENTUCKY)
Sep'39:206

Henderson, David Pat
Letter. Dec'34:279

HENDRICKS, J. T. (PRESBYTERIAN)
    (KENTUCKY)
Oct'38:225

Hendrickson, B. S. (New York)
Letter. Apr'32:95
Letter. Jul'32:167

HENDRICKSON, BENJAMIN (NEW YORK)
Jul'38:160

Henley, Thomas M. (Virginia)
Letter. May'33:118
Letter. Mar'34:68

Henry, John (Ohio)
Letter. Mar'39:71

HENRY, JOHN (OHIO)
Jan'32:24
Feb'32:47
Jan'38:15

HENRY, PHILIP
quoted. Mar'33:60

Henshall, James (Virginia)
Letter. Jun'42:129

HENSHALL, JAMES (VIRGINIA)
Apr'42:81

HENSLEY, B. (INDIANA)
Jan'37C:24

HENSLEY, B. S. (KENTUCKY)
May'42:115

HENSLEY, C. S. (INDIANA)
Jan'37C:24

37

HERETIC DETECTOR
Jul'37C:146
quoted. Sep(ieOct)'37C:193
Mar'38:back cover
quoted. Apr'38:91
Aug'38:185
Oct'38:227
Jul'41:164

HERNDON, D. (VIRGINIA)
Jan'37C:23

HERNDON, F. (KENTUCKY)
Jan'37C:23

HERRON. (OHIO)
Jun'42:140

HEWETT. (ILLINOIS)
May'33:109

HIATT. (VIRGINIA)(MISSOURI)
Jul'40:155

HICKORY, PENNSYLVANIA
Mar'32:71

Hicks, Beverly A. (Kentucky)
Lafayette Seminary. May'40:120

HICKS, BEVERLY A. (KENTUCKY)
Feb'35:45

HIGGINSPORT, KENTUCKY
Jul'42:168

HIGH WAY OF HOLINESS (COLUMBIA,
TENNESSEE)
Aug'38:184

Hill, Milton H
Letter. May'39:113

HILL, ROWLAND
May'33:117

HIMES, JOSHUA V.
Oct'41:238

Himes, Joshua W. (Massachusetts)
Letter. Mar'35:64

HINDUISM
Jan'34:5

HINE'S CREEK, KENTUCKY
Oct(ieSep)'37C:176

HINTON, ISAAC T. (BAPTIST)
(VIRGINIA)
Mar'34:68

HITESVILLE, ILLINOIS
Jan'42:22

Hixon, Nathan (Kentucky)
Letter. Mar'33:66

HOLLINGSWORTH, W. (OHIO)
Jan'37C:23

Holmes, Erastus
Letter. Jul'39:162

HOLTON. (KENTUCKY)
Jan'33:22
Jun'40:144
Oct'41:231

HOLTON, J. (KENTUCKY)
Mar'40:70

Holton, J. M. (Kentucky)
Letter. Oct'33:236
Letter. Jun'42:141
Letter. Jul'42:167

HOLTZCLAW, E. (KENTUCKY)
Jan'37C:23

HOLY SPIRIT
Oct'32:238
Jan'33:5,24
Feb'33:26
Apr'33:77
May'33:97
Jun'33:141,142
Aug'33:191
Sep'33:197,208
Nov'33:255
Dec'33:282
Feb'34:37
Mar'34:64

Apr'34:88
May'34:113
Jun'34:141
Aug'34:174
Oct'34:226,231,
Nov'34:249
Jun'35:133
Aug'35:190
Jun'38:139
Sep'40:195,206
Feb'41:33,45
Mar'42:52
Aug'42:187

HONESTY
Aug'42:192

HOPE
Apr'37C:78
Feb'38:42
Jan'42:5
May'42:98

HOPEWELL, KENTUCKY
Sep'42:215

Hopkins, John M. (Missouri)
Letter. Jan'33:22

HOPKINSVILLE, KENTUCKY
Jan'35:22
Sep'42:215

Howard.
Millennium and second coming of
the Lord.
no. 1. Oct'41:228
no. 2. Nov'41:254
no. 3. Dec'41:277
Short sermon for the "orthodox"
Nov'41:260

Howard, Benjamin (New York)
Letter. Oct'35:220

Howard, John R. (Tennessee)
Progress of the Gospel. May'34:117
Imprudence of a proclaimer.
Jun'37C:121

HOWARD, JOHN R. (TENNESSEE)
Jun'37C:136
quoted. Apr'38:91
Oct'38:225
Jun'42:143

Howard, John S. (Illinois)
Progress of the Gospel. May'34:118

HUBBARD, ALEXANDER
Death. Feb'40:46

HUBBARD, E.
Jan'38:15

Hubbard, E. B. (Ohio)
Letter. Feb'40:45

HUBBARD, SCOTT
Death. Feb'40:46

HUBBELL, E. (OHIO)
Jul'41:166

HUDSON, OHIO
Oct'33:234

HUGHES. (CATHOLIC)
Apr'33:73

Hughes, J. H. (Missouri)
Letter. Sep'33:214

HUGHES, J. H. (MISSOURI)
Sep'33:214

HUGHES, JAMES (INDIANA)
Mar'35:69

HUME, DAVID
Jun'39:121

Hundley, J. S. (Alabama)
Letter. May'40:113

Hunter, W.
The natural man. Apr'37C:81

HUNTER, WILLIAM
May'37C:100
Aug'37C:167
Oct(ieSep)'37C:183
Sep(ieOct)'37C:199

HUNTSVILLE, ALABAMA
Jun'34:132

HURLBUT, C. D.
Apr'41:90

HYATTSTOWN (MONTGOMERY CO.) MARYLAND
Sep'39:207

HYGEIA FEMALE ACADEMY (ATHENEUM)
    (MOUNT HEALTHY, OHIO)
  Sep'39:205
  Oct'39:240
  Jun'42:142
  Nov'42:263

HYGIENE
  Jun'33:124
  May'38:116

HYMNALS
  Feb'39:48   Sep'39:216
  Aug'39:191   Jan'40:20

HYMNODY
  See
  HYMNALS

HYMNS
    See also
  POEMS
  VOCAL MUSIC
  Jan'33:9
  Jan'33:20
  Nov'34:263
  Mar'35:71

I

ICELAND
Jun'33:124

IGANTIUS
Sep(ieOct)'37C:195

ILLINOIS
Aug'32:192
May'33:109
May'34:118
Oct'34:239
Dec'34:279
Jun'35:144
Jul'37C:151
Jan'42:22
Feb'42:44

IMMIGRATION AND EMIGRATION
Aug'35:182

INDEPENDENCE DAY
     See
FOURTH OF JULY

INDEPENDENCE, MISSOURI
Jul'40:154

INDIANA
May'32:119   Aug'37C:167
Aug'32:192   Sep(ieOct)'37C:
Jan'33:24   195
Sep'33:212,214   May'38:103,117,118
Dec'33:283,286   Jul'38:167,168
Feb'34:46,47,48   Aug'38:190,191,192
Apr'34:93   Jan'39:23
May'34:114   Mar'39:71
Jun'34:144   May'39:119
Jul'34:164   Jul'39:163,164
Oct'34:235   Dec'39:284
Dec'34:281   Oct'41:231,232,233
Jan'35:24   Jan'42:21,24
Feb'35:42   May'42:116
Mar'35:69,70   Jun'42:141
Jun'35:144   Jul'42:160
Jan'37C:21   Sep'42:216
May'37C:120

INDIANAPOLIS, INDIANA
Dec'33:283,288
Jan'42:24

INDIANS OF NORTH AMERICA
Jun'35:126

INTEREST AND USURY
May'33:106

THE INVESTIGATOR (JOHN THOMAS)
Oct'41:237

IOWA
Mar'41:71

IRELAND. (LOUISIANA)
May'33:116

IRELAND
Sep'33:215
Sep'42:207

IRENEUS
May'42:100

IRON'S CREEK (OVERTON CO.)
     TENNESSEE
Nov'40:257

IRVIN
     See also
IRWIN

IRVIN. (KENTUCKY)
Apr'38:87
Jun'41:144

IRVIN. (MRS. THOMAS H.) (KENTUCKY)
Death. Jun'38:143

Irvin, J.
Letter. Apr'35:87
A nut for geologists. Aug'40:188
Letter. Oct'40:239

IRVIN, JOSHUA (KENTUCKY)
Sep'33:213
May'38:120
Dec'40:284
Oct'41:223

IRVIN, THOMAS H. (KENTUCKY)
Jun'38:143

Irvin, W. M.
Letter. Aug'33:191

IRVIN, WILLIAM
Jan'33:23

Irvin, William C. (Ohio)
Letter. Jan'33:23

IRWIN
See also
IRVIN

IRWIN, J. (KENTUCKY)
Oct'38:225

Irwin, W. C. (Ohio)
Letter. Aug'42:187

IRWIN, WILLIAM
Oct'38:225

ISAAC (BIBLICAL CHARACTER)
Apr'34:77

ISLAM
Jan'34:9

ISRAELITE (NATHANIEL FIELD)
Aug'41:192
Dec'41:285
quoted. Dec'42:283

J

J., L. H.
The New Testament no text book.
Nov'34:259
Letter. May'38:105

JACKSON COUNTY, MISSOURI
Sep'33:215

JACKSONVILLE, ILLINOIS
May'33:111
Oct'34:239
Jun'35:144

JACOB (BIBLICAL CHARACTER)
Apr'34:78

JAMESON (KENTUCKY)
Aug'40:187
Oct(ieSep)'37C:178

JAMESON, ELIZABETH M.
Obituary. Jul'41:167

Jameson, Love H.
Letter. Jan'35:24
Letter. Aug'35:189
Letter. May'37C:117
Letter. Jul'38:167
Letter. Aug'38:190
Letter. Oct'40:238

JAMESON, LOVE H.
Jun'34:140,144
May'35:109
Jul'35:167
Jan'38:15
May'38:118
Oct'38:229
Jul'41:167

JAMESTOWN, INDIANA
Sep(ieOct)'37C:195

JAMESTOWN, OHIO
Apr'34:96
Jun'42:140

JEFFERSON (HAHTABULA CO.) OHIO
Jan'34:21

JEFFERSON CITY (COLE CO.) MISSOURI
Nov'39:264

JEFFERSONTOWN, KENTUCKY
May'39:119

JEFFERSONVILLE, INDIANA
Oct'34:235
Jul'39:164
May'42:116

JEROME
Feb'40:30

JERUSALEM
Oct'34:221
Oct'39:226,228
Dec'39:268
Jul'41:159
Aug'41:171

JESUS CHRIST
Apr'32:89
May'32:102,104
Oct'32:223
Jan'33:5,17
Feb'33:27
May'33:103
Aug'38:169
Sep'38:199
Oct'38:217
Mar'39:49
Jul'40:152
Jul'41:149
Aug'41:175
May'42:109

JESUS CHRIST--DEATH AND RESURRECTION
Jun'34:130
Oct'34:217
Dec'34:275
Mar'35:49
Apr'35:73
May'35:97,103
Jun'35:121
Jun'38:142
Apr'39:73
Dec'39:271
Jul'40:163

JEWS
Jul'32:150
Aug'32:176
Oct'32:223,230
Dec'32:277
Jan'33:13
May'33:106,112
Dec'33:279
Oct'34:222
Nov'34:241
Sep'35;199,200
May'37C:105
Jul'39:154
Sep'39:193
Oct'39:226,228
Nov'39;249,250
Apr'40:84
May'40:105,112
(cont. next page)

43

JEWS (cont.)
Sep'40:209,211,212 May'42:105
Oct'40:235   Jul'42:145
Jul'41:158   Oct'42:216,221
Aug'41:169,172   Oct'42:229,231
Mar'42:65   Dec'42:267

JOHLSON, J. INSTRUCTION IN THE
    MOSAIC RELIGION
quoted. May'33:106

JOHN THE BAPTIST
May'34:97

JOHNSON. (KENTUCKY)
Jun'41:140

JOHNSON, ALPHEUS (KENTUCKY)
Apr'38:87

JOHNSON, DARWIN (KENTUCKY)
Jun'35:125

JOHNSON, HENRY (KENTUCKY)
Jan'37C:23

JOHNSON, J. (ARKANSAS)
Jan'37C:23

JOHNSON, JAMES (KENTUCKY)
Jan'37C:23

Johnson, John T. (Kentucky)
Progress of Reform. Feb'34:48
Progress of the Gospel.
    Oct'35:239
Bacon College. Jan'37C:19,21
The Christian--what is he?
    Apr'37C:89
Note. Apr'37C:96
Answer to query. May'37C:107
Letter. May'37C:109
Reply. May'37C:115
Conquests of the Gospel. May'37C:
    116
Notices. May'37C:117
Conquests of the Gospel. Jun'37C:
    136
Natural theology.
    Jul'37C:148
    Sep(ieOct)'37C:184

Johnson, John T. (cont.)
Conquests of the Gospel. Jul'37C
    151
To the patrons of the Christian.
    Aug'37C:166
Bacon College. Aug'37C:166
Notices. Aug'37C:167
Sucess of the Gospel--extraordina
    Oct(ieSep)'37C:176,177,178
Mr. Stiles, again. Oct(ieSep)
    '37C:181
(News) Sep(ieOct)'37C:199
Extraordinary success of the
    true Gospel. Jan'38:24
Letter. Feb'38:48
Historical sketch of a protracted
    meeting... Apr'38:85
Protracted meeting at Georgetown,
    Kentucky. Apr'38:87
Observations on the Union of Bro.
    Bosworth. Apr'38:89
Letter. May'38:117
Letter. Aug'38:192
Letter. Sep'38:211
Conversions. Oct'38:233
Letter. Dec'38:266
News. Jan'39:23
Letter. Mar'39:70
Letter. May'39:119
Letter. Jul'39:162,163,164
Letter. Sep'39:205,209
Letter. Oct'39:236
Letter. Dec'39:284
Letter. Mar'40:69
Letter. Apr'40:95
Letter. May'40:114
Letter. Jun'40:142
Letter. Aug'40:191
Letter. Sep'40:215
Letter. Nov'40:258
Letter. Dec'40:284
Letter. Jan'41:23
Letter. Mar'41:70
Letter. Jun'41:140
Letter. Aug'41:190
Letter. Jan'42:23
Letter. Feb'42:45
Progress of Reform. May'42:116
Letter. Jun'42:139,140
Female Collegiate Institute.
    Aug'42:186
(cont. next page)

Johnson, John T. (cont.)
 Letter. Sep'42:215
 Letter. Oct'42:239

JOHNSON, JOHN T.
 Feb'32:30   quoted. Sep'38:
 May'33:110   210
 Sep'33:211   Oct'38:235
 Oct'33:238   Jan'39:23,24
 Jun'34:144   Mar'39:72
 Jul'34:159   May'40:101,114,117
 Sep'34:195,204   Jun'40:144
 Oct'34:226   Sep'40:213
 Nov'34:264   Oct'40:217
 Jan'35:21   Dec'40:284
 Feb'35:45   Jan'41:23
 May'35:113   Jun'41:127
 Jun'35:126   Aug'41:189
 Jan'37C:23   Oct'41:231
 Jun'37C:135   Dec'41:286
 Jan'38:22   Jan'42:21
 Jun'38:128,144   May'42:115,117
 Jul'38:145,168

JOHNSON, LYMAN
 Oct'38:227

JOHNSON, MARY (KENTUCKY)
 Apr'38:87

JOHNSON, RICHARD M. (KENTUCKY)
 Jun'35:126

JOHNSON, T. (KENTUCKY)
 Jan'37C:23

Johnson, Thomas C. (Indiana)
 Letter. Mar'35:69

JOHNSON, THOMAS C. (INDIANA)
 Sep'33:214
 Mar'34:72

Johnson, Thornton F.
 Letter. Jan'37C:12
 Female Collegiate Institute
     Jan'38:inside front cover
     Mar'38:inside back cover
     Oct'38:233

JOHNSON, THORNTON F.
 May'35:113

JOHNSON, THORNTON .F. (cont.)
 Jan'37C:19,23
 May'37C:109
 Aug'37C:167
 Oct(ieSep)'37C:183
 May'38:120
 Feb'41:47
 Nov'42:262

JOHNSTOWN, PENNSYLVANIA
 Sep(ieOct)'37C:193

JONES. (KENTUCKY)
 Oct'41:231

JONES. (OHIO)
 Apr'33:95

JONES, F. (KENTUCKY)
 Jan'37C:23

JONES, JOHN L. (INDIANA)
 Jun'34:144
 Feb'35:42

Jones, John T.
 Letter. May'33:109
 Letter. Dec'34:279
 Letter. Jul'35:166

JONES, JOHN T.
 Dec'34:282
 May'40:101

Jones, Josiah (Ohio)
 History of the Mormonites.
     Jun'41:132

JONES, S. F. (MISSOURI)
 Nov'39:263

Jourdan, W. D.
 Methodist preacher converted.
     Dec'41:286
 New birth. Jul'42:152

JOURDAN, W. D.
 May'37C:106
 quoted. Jun'37C:135,136

JOURNAL OF CHRISTIANITY
  Jun'40:144
  Nov'40:259
  Jul'41:164

JOURNAL OF LITERARY INSTITUTIONS
  quoted. Feb'32:37
  quoted. Mar'32:67
  quoted. Jun'32:136
  quoted. Aug'32:185

JOURNALISM
    See also
  PERIODICALS
  Jan'32:20

JOY AND SORROW
  Aug'41:191

JUDAISM
    See also
  JEWS

JUDAISM (cont.)
  Jan'34:9
  Jun'34:139
  Sep'35:200
  Oct'35:224

JUDD, ROSWELL (INDIANA)
  May'38:104

JUDEA
  Sep'40:211

JUDGEMENT
  Apr'38:91
  Feb'39:27

JUSTIN MARTYR
  May'42:100
  Sep'(ieOct)'37C:197

Juvenis
  Guizott on civilization. Nov'39:2
  What is civilization? Mar'40:67

K

., A. D. (Kentucky)
Letter. Jun'40:144

.., W. A. (Kentucky)
Virtue. Oct'38:220

ELLEY, J. (KENTUCKY)
Jan''37C:23

ELSO, ISAAC
Dec'41:286

EMPTON, JOSEPH (INDIANA)
May'38:104

ENDRICK. (ALABAMA)
May'40:113

ENDRICK. (KENTUCKY)
May'40:101
Aug'41:190

ENDRICK, A. (KENTUCKY)
Oct'40:218
Oct'41:223
Jan'42:21,23
Jun'42:139

ENDRICK, C. (KENTUCKY)
Feb'42:46
Jun'42:139

ENDRICK, CARROL
Aug'41:190
Oct'41:231

ENSONTOWN, KENTUCKY
Sep'33:213

ENTUCKY

Feb'32:30,47	Jan'33:22
Mar'32:71	Sep'33:213,214
Apr'32:95	Oct'33:236
May'32:112	Jan'34:23,24
Jun'32:139,142	Feb'34:46,47
Jul'32:166	Apr'34:93
Aug'32:192	Jul'34:164
Sep'32:213,214,215	Dec'34:281
Oct'32:239	Jan'35:21,22,23

KENTUCKY (cont.)
May'35:109
Jun'35:123
Aug'35:189
Oct'35:239
Jan'37C:11,20,21
Apr'37C:92,93,96
May'37C:106,115
May'37C:116,117
Jun'37C:133,135,136
Jul'37C:151,152
Aug'37C:167
Oct(ieSep)'37C:176,177
Sep(ieOct)'37C:199
Jan'38:24
Feb'38:48
Apr'38:85,87
May'38:115,117,118,119,120
Jun'38:143,144
Jul'38:168
Aug'38:192
Sep'38:210
Oct'38:232,233
Dec'38:266
Jan'39:23,24
Mar'39:72
May'39:119
Jul'39:153,161,162,163,164,167
Aug'39:190,191
Sep'39:204,205,206,207,209
Oct'39:236
Dec'39:284
Feb'40:46
Mar'40:63,69,72
Apr'40:95,96
May'40:100,114,117,118
Jun'40:144
Jul'40:146
Aug'40:191
Sep'40:213,215,216
Oct'40:217
Nov'40:258
Dec'40:284
Jan'41:23
Mar'41:70
Apr'41:96
May'41:119,120
Jun'41:127,140,144
(cont. next page)

KENTUCKY (cont.)
 Jul'41:162
 Aug'41:189,190
 Sep'41:215
 Oct'41:223,231,232,233
 Dec'41:282,283,286
 Jan'42:21,23
 Feb'42:41,45,46
 May'42:115,116,117
 Jun'42:139,140,141,142
 Jul'42:167,168
 Aug'42:189
 Sep'42:215,216
 Oct'42:239
 Nov'42:262
 Dec'42:283

KEYES (KENTUCKY)
 May'35:110

KIMMONT, ALEX. (OHIO)
 Aug'33:192

KINCHELOW, S. (KENTUCKY)
 Jan'37C:23

KINCHELOW, T. W. (KENTUCKY)
 Jan'37C:23

King, Julia A.
 Obituary of Susan King. Sep'39:213

KING, SUSAN
 Obituary. Sep'39:213

KING, W. (OHIO)
 Jan'37C:23

KINGDOM OF GOD
     See also
 MILLENNIUM
 PROVIDENCE AND GOVERNMENT OF GOD

KINGDOM OF GOD
 May'34:97,104
 Jun'34:121
 Dec'34:271
 Feb'40:41
 Jan'41:5
 Feb'41:25
 Mar'41:49,60
 Apr'41:73,84
 May'41:97
 Jul'41:154
 Aug'41:169
 Nov'41:241

KINGS AND RULERS
 May'32:120

KINGS CREEK, VIRGINIA
 Feb'34:48

KINNE, S. (NEW YORK)
 Jan'37C:23

KNIGHT, W. (KENTUCKY)
 Jan'37C:23

Kyes, Alvin
 Letter. Apr'33:95

L

LAFAYETTE SEMINARY (KENTUCKY)
Feb'35:45
May'40:120

LAMSON, J. R. (INDIANA)
Feb'40:47

LANCASTER. (KENTUCKY)
Oct'35:239

LANCASTER. (MISSOURI)
Jul'40:156
Apr'41:95

LANCASTER, J. P. (MISSOURI)
Nov'39:263
May'42:117

LANCASTER, KENTUCKY
Feb'42:46

Lanphear, Wesley (Pennsylvania)
Item of ecclesiastical intelligence.
    Sep(ieOct)'37C:193

Lantham, C. N.
Letter. Apr'34:93

LATHAM, DANIEL (NORTH CAROLINA)
Jun'40:140

Latham, Thomas J. (North Carolina)
Progress of Reform. Mar'34:71
Letter. Jun'40:140

Latimer, J. B. (Kentucky)
Letter. May'42:115

LAW. (INDIANA)
Oct'41:223
Jun'42:142

LAW, THOMAS (D.C.)
Jan'37C:23

LAW
Feb'32:34

LAW SCHOOLS
Jul'32:168

LAWRENCEBURGH, ?
Sep'33:212

LAWRENCEBURGH, KENTUCKY
Jun'42:139

LAWRENCEVILLE, ILLINOIS
May'34:118

LAWSON. (KENTUCKY)
Sep'40:216

Layton, P. S. (Kentucky)
Letter. Jul'39:161

LEE, W. (MISSOURI)
May'42:118

LEESBURGH, KENTUCKY
Sep'38:210
Dec'38:266
Sep'39:205
Jun'41:144
Sep'42:215

LEMISDEN, WILLIAM (ENGLAND)
Jul'38:162

LENOIR, W. A. (TENNESSEE)
Jan'37C:23

Leonard, Silas W.
Sacred music.
    Aug'38:186
    no. 1. Oct'39:233
    no. 2. Nov'39:252

LEONARD, SILAS W.
Sep'38:214

Levi, David
The end and purpose to be effected
    by the Resurrection. May'33:11

LEVI, DAVID
quoted. Oct'32:226

LEWIS, SAMUEL
Jan'37C:18

Lewis, William W. (Tennessee)
Letter. Apr'34:94

LEXINGTON, KENTUCKY
Feb'32:30   Mar'40:65
Jun'35:125   Oct'40:217
Apr'37C:92   May'41:119
Aug'37C:167   Jun'41:127
Aug'38:192   Jun'42:140

LEXINGTON, MISSOURI
Jul'40:154

Liberator
Letter on slavery. Jun'35:136
Letter. Jul'35:150
Letter. Aug'35:174

LIBERATOR
Jun'35:144
Oct'35:238

LIBERIA
May'33:116

LIBERTY, KENTUCKY
Aug'37C:167

LIBERTY, MISSOURI
Jul'40:155

LIBERTY, OHIO
Jan'37C:11

LIBRARIES
Jan'42:12

LIMESTONE, ALABAMA
Sep'34:216

LINCOLN, KENTUCKY
Sep'39:209

LINDSEY, N. L. (KENTUCKY)
Death. Oct'40:239

LIQUOR
See
TEMPERANCE

Litch, J.
Letter. Jul'42:155

LITERATURE
Jun'32:136
Aug'32:185

Littell, A. (Indiana)
Progress of Reform. Feb'34:46
Letter to Dr. Nathaniel Field
on slavery. Feb'35:39

LITTLE FLAT ROCK, INDIANA
Dec'33:287

LITTLE GROVE, ILLINOIS
Jan'42:22

LITTLE KENTUCK, PENNSYLVANIA
Sep(ieOct)'37C:193

LOGAN, INDIANA
May'38:103

LONG HORSELY, ENGLAND
Dec'42:282

LONGLEY, ABNER H.
Mar'33:66

LONGLEY, J. (INDIANA)
Sep'33:213

LORD'S DAY
See
SUNDAY

LORD'S SUPPER
Mar'33:72
Oct'35:218
Apr'38:88
Aug'40:174

LORDSTOWN, OHIO
Sep'32:215

LOUISIANA
Jun'32:143
Aug'32:192
Feb'42:47

LOUISVILLE BEREAN AND BIBLICAL
INTERPRETER
Mar'38:68
Aug'38:189

LOUISVILLE HERALD
  quoted. Jun'33:126

LOUISVILLE, KENTUCKY
  Jan'34:23,24
  Feb'34:47
  Jan'37C:21
  Sep'(ieOct)'37C:199
  Jul'39:162,163
  Aug'39:191
  Mar'40:72
  Jan'42:23

LOUTRE (AUDRAIN CO.) MISSOURI
  Nov'39:263

LOVE
  Jan'35:21
  Aug'37C:167

LOVE FEAST
  Apr'41:90

LOVEJOY, H. (OHIO)
  Dec'41:285

LUCAS. (KENTUCKY)
  Dec'41:284

LUCAS, J. B.
  Oct'38:231
  Jan'41:23
  Dec'41:285

Lucy.
  Letter. Sep'32:214

LUCY, GEORGE (OHIO)
  Dec'33:284
  Jan'38:15

LUCY, J. (OHIO)
  Sep'32:215

LUDLOW, JAMES
  Sep'38:208

LUDLOW'S, KENTUCKY
  Sep'40:216

LUNENBURGH, VIRGINIA
  May'42:117

LYNCH, J. B. (SOUTH CAROLINA)
  Jan'37C:23

Lynd, Samuel W.
  On baptism. Nov'33:242

LYND, SAMUEL W.
  Sep'33:193
  Oct'33:217
  Nov'33:241,247
  Dec'33:266
  Feb'34:29
  Apr'34:82
  May'34:110
  Apr'38:94

51

M

M., J. M.
Query. May'37C:107

MC BRIDE, THOMAS (MISSOURI)
Jul'40:154
May'42:118

McCall, J. R. (Kentucky)
Letter. Sep'33:211
Letter. Jan'35:22

MCCALL, J. R. (KENTUCKY)
May'34:116

MCCALL, JOHN R. (LOUISIANA)
Sep'40:216

MCCANN, J. W. (KENTUCKY)
Sep'33:214

MCCLENAHAN. (MARYLAND)
Sep'39:207

McClenahan, William
Letter. Jan'34:22

MCCOWN, BURR (METHODIST) (KENTUCKY)
Mar'40:69
Jun'40:144

MACEDONIA, KENTUCKY
Jun'42:140

McElroy, James (Pennsylvania)
Letter. Feb'32:47
Reflections on the death of a
    brother (poem) Aug'32:191
Letter. Apr'33:94

MCELROY, JOHN (PENNSYLVANIA)
Aug'32:190

MCFARLAND, WALTER
Mar'35:68

McGee, John (Indiana)
Letter. Dec'33:283

MCGUFFY, ALEXANDER
May'37C:100

MCHATTON, F. (KENTUCKY)
Jan'37C:23

MCHATTON, WILLIAM (KENTUCKY)
Jan'37C:23

MACK, ROBERT (TENNESSEE)
Aug'38:184

MCKEESPORT, PENNSYLVANIA
Sep'33:216

MCKENDREE, W. (METHODIST)
Jun'38:137

MCKEVER, MATTHEW (PENNSYLVANIA)
Feb'39:48

MCLELLEN, WILLIAM
Oct'38:226

M'Neely. (Ohio)
Letter. Apr'32:95

McNeely, Cyrus (Ohio)
Letter. Dec'33:283

MCVEY.
Jan'34:22

MAHONING ASSOCIATION
Feb'32:40

MAINE
Apr'32:96

MALEDICTION
    See
CURSES

MAN
Jul'41:167

MAN (THEOLOGY)
Jan'32:1
Apr'37C:81
May'37C:117
Jul'42:153

MANCHESTER, NEW YORK
  Jan'33:22

MANSFIELD, D. (OHIO)
  May'37C:100

MANSFIELD, OHIO
  May'34:115
  Feb'35:42

MANTUA, OHIO
  Feb'35:43

MARGERUM, J. (KENTUCKY)
  Jan'37C:24

MARION (GRANT CO.) INDIANA
  May'39:119

MARRIAGE
  Nov'32:245
  Dec'32:265,269
  Feb'35:40
  Jun'35:135
  Jun'40:140
  Oct'40:227
  Dec'40:272
  Jan'41:11
  Feb'41:39

MARSHALL. (KENTUCKY)
  Sep'39:206

MARSHALL, S. G.
  Jul'37C:151
  Sep(ieOct)'37C:199

MARTIN, J. G. (KENTUCKY)
  Sep'33:214

Martin, Warnick (Ohio)
  Progress of the Gospel. Sep'35:215
  Letter. Dec'35:283

MARYLAND
  Jun'32:144   Feb'35:42
  Mar'33:72   Dec'38:288
  Jan'34:23   Sep'39:207
  Mar'34:71   Nov'40:255
  Apr'34:95   Dec'40:282
  Aug'34:192   Jan'41:23

MARYLAND (cont.)
  Jul'41:161
  Apr'42:74
  May'42:113

MASON, GILBERT (BAPTIST) (KENTUCKY)
  Jul'37C:139

MASON, KENTUCKY
  Jan'41:23

MASON'S SACRED HARP
  Feb'39:48

MASONS
    See
  FREEMASONS

MASSACHUSETTS
  Apr'32:96
  May'33:116
  Feb'34:47
  Aug'38:191
  Nov'40:256

MATERIALISM
  Jul'40:156

Mathes, James M. (Indiana)
  Exposition of 1st Corinthians
    15:29. Jun'42:127

MATHES, JAMES M. (INDIANA)
  Aug'37C:167

MATTHEWS, J. M. (INDIANA)
  Oct'41:232

Matthews, James M. (Indiana)
  Letter. Aug'38:192
  Letter. Jul'39:161

MATTHEWS, T. J. (OHIO)
  Aug'33:192

Matthews, W. E. (Mississippi)
  Letter. Apr'33:94

MAVITY, JESSE (INDIANA)
  Death. Oct'40:238

MAYSLICK, KENTUCKY

Mar'32:71	Jul'37C:151
May'32:112	Apr'38:87
Jun'32:139	May'38:119
Jul'32:166	Jan'39:23
Oct'32:239	Jan'41:23
Jan'34:23	Mar'41:70
Jan'35:23	Jun'41:140
Jun'37C:136	

MAYSVILLE, KENTUCKY
Jun'37C:136
Jun'38:143
Oct'39:237
Jan'41:23
Nov'42:262

MEAD, EDWARD (METHODIST)
May'35:108

MEDICAL SCHOOLS
Jul'32:168

MEDICINE
Aug'42:169

MEETING HOUSES
    See
CHURCH BUILDINGS

MENTOR, OHIO
May'40:113

MENTZEL, HENRY (MARYLAND)
Dec'40:283

Merriwether, Charles (Kentucky)
  Progress of the Gospel. Oct'35:239

MESSIAH
 Jan'32:6
 Apr'34:75

METCALF, T. (TENNESSEE)
 Jan'37C:23

METEORS
 Feb'34:44

METHODISTS

Mar'33:62	May'35:108
May'33:109,117	Jun'37C:133

METHODISTS (cont.)

Jun'38:137	Sep'39:204
Oct'38:231	Mar'40:69
May'39:113	May'40:112,11
Jul'39:154	Oct'40:225
Aug'39:190	Jan'42:22

MIAMITOWN, OHIO
 Oct'41:231

MICHIGAN
 Aug'32:192
 Dec'42:276

MICROSCOPES
 Oct'40:221

MIDDLEBURGH, OHIO
 Oct'33:234

MIDDLETOWN, INDIANA
 Jan'42:22

MIDDLETOWN, KENTUCKY
 May'39:119

MILLENNIAL HARBINGER
 Oct'33:235
 quoted. Feb'34:45
 Sep'34:202
 quoted. Oct(ieSep)'37C:178
 Feb'38:45
 quoted. Mar'38:back cover
 quoted. May'38:116
 quoted. Oct'39:230
 Jul'40:157
 Aug'40:172
 Sep'40:201
 Nov'40:241
 quoted. Jan'41:23
 Jul'41:164
 May'42:118

MILLENNIUM

Jan'32:24	Oct'34:219
Feb'32:40,44	Nov'34:241
Apr'32:73	Feb'35:33
Jun'32:121	Mar'35:55
Apr'33:88	Apr'35:95,96
Jun'34:133	May'35:114
Jul'34:145	Jul'35:153,15
Aug'34:169	(cont. next p

MILLENNIUM (cont.)

Sep'35:199	Jan'42:5
Apr'38:73	May'42:97,100
Aug'38:174	Jun'42:121,136
Nov'40:245	Jul'42:150,154
Mar'41:62	Aug'42:174,190
Apr'41:84	Sep'42:199,205
Jun'41:142,144	Oct'42:234,236
Jul'41:145,146,147	Nov'42:241,244
Jul'41:154,156	Nov'42:245,247
Aug'41:176	Nov'42:258,261
Oct'41:217,228	Nov'42:262
Nov'41:241,249,254	Dec'42:267,272
Dec'41:265,269,277	Dec'42:275
Dec'41:280,281	

Miller, William (Millennialist)
    (New York)
  Lecture. Aug'42:174

MILLER, WILLIAM (MILLENNIALIST)
    (NEW YORK)
  Jun'41:144
  Aug'41:176
  Oct'41:238
  Jul'42:154
  Aug'42:190
  Sep'42:199
  Dec'42:275

MILLERSBURGH, KENTUCKY

Sep'33:213,214	Sep'39:205
Feb'38:48	Oct'39:236
Apr'38:85,87	Oct'40:221
May'38:118	Dec'40:284
Oct'38:232	

MILLERSBURG (CALLOWAY CO.) MISSOURI
  Nov'39:263
  Apr'41:95

MILTON. (OHIO)
  Apr'33:95

MILTON, JOHN
  Jun'38:130

MILTON, S. K. (KENTUCKY)
  Sep'33:213

MILTON TOWNSHIP (JEFFERSON CO.)
    INDIANA
  Apr'34:93

MINERVA, KENTUCKY
  May'37C:106
  Mar'40:69
  Dec'41:282,284
  Jun'42:141
  Oct'42:239

MINERVA, OHIO
  Dec'35:284

MINISTERS
    See
  CLERGY

MIRACLES
  Dec'35:269
  Jun'39:121

MISSIONS
  May'33:120
  Feb'35:44
  Sep(ieOct)'37C:198
  Jan'40:15
  Apr'40:84

MISSISSIPPI
  Aug'32:192
  Sep'32:214
  Dec'34:282

MISSOURI

Aug'32:192	Jul'40:154
Jan'33:22	Sep'40:216
May'33:111	Apr'41:95
Sep'33:213,214,215	Jul'41:165,166
Dec'34:282	Sep'41:214
Oct'39:238	Oct'41:230
Nov'39:263	May'42:117

MITCHELL. (OHIO)
  Jan'35:24
  Sep(ieOct)'37C:194

Mitchell, James (Ohio)
  Letter. Oct'33:237

MITCHELL, JAMES (OHIO)
  Feb'35:47
  Dec'38:277

MITCHELL'S AMERICAN SYSTEM OF STANDARD
    SCHOOL GEOGRAPHY
  Oct'41:238

MOHAMMED
May'38:107

MOHAMMEDISM
    See
ISLAM

MOMIERISM
Apr'34:95

Monroe, D. (New York)
Letter. Sep'39:206

MONTHLY CHRONICLE
quoted. Jan'40:22

MONTICELLO, KENTUCKY
Sep'39:205

MONTICELLO, MISSOURI
Sep'41:214

MOODY.
Jan'38:15

Moody, George (Massachusetts)
Letter. Nov'40:255

Mooklar, William B.
Letter. Jun'42:141
Letter. Oct'42:239

MOORE. (KENTUCKY)
Oct'40:221

Moore, Gabriel B.
Progress of the Gospel. May'34:
    115
Letter. Jul'34:164

MOORE, J. (PENNSYLVANIA)
quoted. Sep'33:216

MOORSVILLE, ALABAMA
May'40:113

MORGANTOWN (MORGAN CO.) INDIANA
Oct'41:232

MORLEY, ISAAC
Jun'41:133

MORMONS
    See also
    BOOK OF MORMON
Sep'33:215   Jan'41:17
Sep'34:216   May'41:111
Jan'35:22   Jun'41:132
Oct'38:226   Jul'41:165
Jul'39:158   Feb'42:32

MORNING WATCH
Feb'38:47
Aug'38:185
Jul'41:164

MORRIS, THOMAS A. (METHODIST)
quoted. Aug'34:174

MORROW, W. (KENTUCKY)
Oct'41:223

MORTON. (KENTUCKY)
Jul'37C:151
Oct'40:220
May'42:115

MORTON, JOHN (KENTUCKY)
Oct(ieSep)'37C:176

Morton, William (Kentucky)
Success of the Gospel. Jan'37C:2

MORTON, WILLIAM (KENTUCKY)
Feb'34:48   May'39:119
Oct(ieSep)'37C: Sep'39:206
    183   Aug'41:190
Sep(ieOct)'37C: May'42:116
    199   Jun'42:142
Jun'38:144   Oct'42:239
Mar'39:70

MORTONVILLE, KENTUCKY
May'42:116

MOSES
Apr'32:89
May'32:104

MOSES, J. (KENTUCKY)
Jan'37C:23

MOSS. (KENTUCKY)
 Mar'40:69
 Aug'40:187
 Oct'40:220
 Dec'41:284

MOSS. (NEW YORK)
 Apr'34:94

MOSS. (OHIO)
 Aug'33:190
 Sep'39:205
 Mar'41:72

MOSS, I.
 Jan'38:15

MOSS, J. J. (KENTUCKY)
 quoted. Apr'37C:81
 May'40:101
 Jun'40:144
 Jul'40:147

MOTHERS
 Nov'34:262

MOUNT CARMEL, KENTUCKY
 Jun'41:144

MOUNT EDEN, KENTUCKY
 May'42:115

MOUNT HEALTHY, OHIO
 Oct'41:233

MOUNT MORIA (HOWARD CO.) MISSOURI
 Nov'39:263

MOUNT PLEASANT, INDIANA
 Jan'42:21

MOUNT PLEASANT (HOWARD CO.) MISSOURI
 Nov'39:263

MOUNT PLEASANT, OHIO
 Mar'41:72

MOUNT PLEASANT, PENNSYLVANIA
 Mar'35:68

MOUNT STERLING, KENTUCKY
 Sep'39:209
 Aug'41:190
 Jan'42:23

MOUNT TABOR (CALLOWAY CO.)
     MISSOURI
 Nov'39:263

MOUNT VERNON, KENTUCKY
 Jan'35:21
 Oct'35:239
 Oct'38:233
 Jan'39:23
 Dec'39:284

MOUNTAINS
 Mar'35:71

MUDDY (RANDOLPH CO.) MISSOURI
 Nov'39:264

MULETAN. (KENTUCKY)
 May'40:101

MULKEY, J. (KENTUCKY)
 Dec'39:284

MULLINS, SAMUEL G. (KENTUCKY)
 Jan'37C:23
 Aug'37C:167
 Oct(ieSep)'37C:183
 Sep'39:205
 Jul'40:148

MUNFORDSVILLE, KENTUCKY
 Jun'37C:136

MUNROE, DANIEL (NEW YORK)
 Apr'42:83
 quoted. May'42:116

MUNSON, OHIO
 Sep'39:205

MURFREESBORO, TENNESSEE
 Jun'32:140

N

THE NAME CHRISTIAN
    See
CHRISTIAN AS A NAME

THE NAME CHRISTIAN DISCIPLES
    See
CHRISTIAN DISCIPLES AS A NAME

THE NAME DISCIPLES OF CHRIST
    See
DISCIPLES OF CHRIST AS A NAME

THE NAME SERVANT
    See
SERVANT AS A NAME

NAMES, PERSONAL
  Aug'39:184

NAPLES, ITALY
  Oct(ieSep)'37C:174

NAPOLEON BONAPARTE
  May'42:109

NASHVILLE, TENNESSEE
  Sep'32:213
  May'40:112

NATURAL RELIGION
  Mar'32:63
  Jun'32:128
  Apr'35:91
  May'35:116
  Jul'35:152
  Jul'37C:148
  Sep(ieOct)'37C:184

NATURE
  Feb-Mar'37C:54
  Mar'39:69
  Jun'39:121

NAZAREENS
  Nov'35:255

NEAL, J. (KENTUCKY)
  Jan'37C:24

Nelson, William A. (Ohio)
  Letter. Nov'34:261

NESTORIANS
  Mar'42:65

Nevins, (Dr.)
  Heaven's attractions.
    Mar'38:52

Nevins, William
  Thoughts on Popery. May'37C:113

NEW. (INDIANA)
  Jul'34:164

NEW ALBANY, INDIANA
  Jan'37C:21
  May'37C:120
  Jul'39:163

NEW BRUNSWICK
  Oct'41:233

NEW CASTLE (HENRY CO.) KENTUCKY
  Aug'35:189
  Oct'40:220
  Jun'42:139

NEW ENGLAND
    See also states in New England
  Jul'41:164

NEW HAMPSHIRE
  Apr'32:96

NEW IRELAND, KENTUCKY
  Jul'39:161

NEW JERSEY
  Jun'32:144
  Dec'38:288

THE NEW JERUSALEM
    See
HEAVEN
KINGDOM OF GOD

NEW LISBON, OHIO
Apr'33:95
Sep'35:215
May'40:113

NEW MONTHLY MAGAZINE
Oct'34:240

NEW ORLEANS, LOUISIANA
Jun'32:143

NEW PARIS, OHIO
Aug'42:189

NEW RICHMOND, KENTUCKY
Jul'42:168

NEW YEAR
Jan'35:1

NEW YORK
Apr'32:95,96   Sep'34:216
Jul'32:167   Jan'35:21
Sep'32:215   May'35:118
Jan'33:22   Oct'35:221
Aug'33:190   Dec'38:288
Feb'34:47   Jul'41:164
Apr'34:94   Apr'42:83
Jun'34:144   May'42:113,116

NEW YORK, NEW YORK
Jul'38:155
Dec'38:288
Apr'42:83
May'42:113,116

NEW YORK AURORA
quoted. Nov'42:250

NEW YORK COMMERCIAL
quoted. Oct'40:240

NEW YORK EVANGELIST
quoted. Jul'32:165

NEW YORK JOURNAL OF COMMERCE
quoted. Aug'35:183

NEWCASTLE, KENTUCKY
May'37C:116

Newton, John
The Olney Kite (poem) May'35:120

NEWVILLE, OHIO
Feb'35:42

NICHOLASVILLE, KENTUCKY
Oct'33:236
Jan'38:24
Apr'38:87
Oct'40:217

Nicklin, Levi O. C.
Mormonism in Pittsburgh.
Feb'42:32

NICOLAITANS
Nov'35:255

NILES, M. A. H. (INDIANA)
Aug'33:192

Noah, M. M.
Restoration of the Jews.
Sep'40:209

NOBLESTOWN, PENNSYLVANIA
Aug'32:190

NOBLESVILLE, INDIANA
Mar'35:70

NORTH CAROLINA
Jun'32:144
Mar'34:71
Dec'34:282

NORTH LIBERTY, KENTUCKY
Jun'42:141

NORTH MIDDLETOWN, KENTUCKY
Jul'32:166
Sep'33:214
Apr'38:85,87
Nov'40:258
Dec'40:284
Aug'41:190
Jan'42:23

NORTH WESTERN PASSAGE
Jul'40:168

NORTHERN REFORMER, HERETIC DETECTOR
AND EVANGELICAL REVIEW (OHIO)
See also
HERETIC DETECTOR
May'37C:100

NORTON, HERMAN
Jan'37C:18

Norton, J. (England)
Letter. Dec'42:282

NUCKOLLS. (KENTUCKY)
Oct'40:220

NUCKOLLS, G. (KENTUCKY)
Jan'37C:24

NUCKOLLS, G. W. (KENTUCKY)
Jan'37C:23

NUCKOLLS, SAMUEL (KENTUCKY)
Jan'37C:23

An Observer
Order. Jul'40:161
Puffing. Jul'40:162

ODD FELLOWS
Aug'38:192

OHIO

Feb'32:47	Jul'38:167,168
Apr'32:95	Aug'38:191,192
Jun'32:142,143	Sep'38:213
Jul'32:165,167	Oct'38:229
Aug'32:192	Jan'39:23,24
Sep'32:214,215	Mar'39:71,72
Oct'32:239	May'39:119
Jan'33:24	Sep'39:205,208
Apr'33:95	Oct'39:237
Aug'33:190	Feb'40:41
Oct'33:233,238	Mar'40:72
Dec'33:283,284,287	Apr'40:75,96
Jan'34:21	May'40:113
Feb'34:46,47	Aug'40:187,192
Mar'34:71	Sep'40:216
Apr'34:94,96	Nov'40:257,263
May'34:114,115	Dec'40:276
Jun'34:140,144	Mar'41:72
Jul'34:165	Apr'41:95
Aug'34:192	May'41:120
Nov'34:261	Jul'41:166
Dec'34:281	Sep'41:216
Jan'35:21,24	Oct'41:230,231,233
Feb'35:42,43,44	Apr'42:73
Feb'35:46	Jun'42:140,141
Mar'35:72	Jul'42:168
Jul'35:167	Aug'42:190
Aug'35:189,190,192	Sep'42:215,216
Sep'35:215	Dec'42:284
Oct'35:240	
Dec'35:283	
Jan'37C:11	
May'37C:106,117	
Jul'37C:151,152	
Oct(ieSep)'37C:177	
Sep(ieOct)'37C:194	
Jan'38:11,22	
Mar'38:57	
Apr'38:90	
May'38:103,115,117	

OHIO MEDICAL COLLEGE
Aug'35:192

O'Kane, John
Circular. Dec'33:285
Letter. Dec'39:284

O'KANE, JOHN

Sep'33:212	May'38:104
Oct'33:240	Aug'38:190
Jul'34:164	Jan'39:23
Dec'34:281	Oct'41:231
Jan'35:23	Jan'42:22
Feb'35:42	
Oct(ieSep)'37C:178	

OLD BETHEL, KENTUCKY
Oct'42:239

An Old Christian
Downfall of Babylon the Great.
Jan'42:17

Orange, Daniel (Illinois)
Letter. Feb'42:44

ORDER OF WORSHIP
May'35:111
Jul'38:157

ORDINATIONS OF BISHOPS
Jul'39:161
Mar'41:72

ORDINATIONS OF ELDERS
Apr'32:95
Mar'41:72

ORIGINAL SIN
Jun'33:133

OSBURN. (SISTER) (PENNSYLVANIA)
Aug'32:190

OVERTON, TENNESSEE
Jan'39:24

OVINGTON, WILLIAM (NEW YORK)
Jul'38:160

OWEN, (KENTUCKY)
 May'40:101

Owen, E. (Ohio)
 Letter. Dec'33:284

OWEN, ROBERT. DEBATE WITH A.
     CAMPBELL
 Jan'35:24

OWEN, ROBERT DALE
 Apr'32:76

Owen, Thomas
 "The Gospel Restored" Jan'38:23
 Letter. Feb'42:45

OWENTON, KENTUCKY
 Aug'37C:167

OXFORD, INDIANA
 Sep'33:212

OXFORD, OHIO
 Dec'33:287
 Jan'38:103

P

P
Reformation publications. Aug'39:189

P., O.
Conversion.
    Jun'40:135
    Jul'40:150

PADGET. (KENTUCKY)
May'38:115

PADGET. (OHIO)
Apr'41:96
Jun'42:140
Dec'42:284

Padget, George W.
Letter. Jul'42:168

PADGET, GEORGE W. (OHIO)
Oct'41:231

PAGE, JOHN E. (MORMON)
Feb'42:33

PAINE, S. B. (GEORGIA)
Jan'37C:24

PAINEVILLE (AMELIA CO.) VIRGINIA
Mar'39:67

PALESTINE
Dec'39:268

PALMER. (ILLINOIS)
Jul'35:166

PALMER, F. R. (MISSOURI)
Jul'40:154

PALMER, H. D. (ILLINOIS)
May'34:118

PALMYRA (HENRY CO.) KENTUCKY
May'37C:116
Oct'40:220

PALMYRA, MISSOURI
Sep'40:216

PARABLES
Feb'34:25
May'34:98
Jun'34:121

PARIS, ILLINOIS
Jan'42:22

PARIS, KENTUCKY
Sep'33:214
Jan'38:24
Feb'38:48
Apr'38:87
May'38:118
Nov'40:258
Dec'40:284
Oct'41:223

PARIS (MONROE CO.) MISSOURI
Nov'39:263
Sep'40:216
Sep'41:214
Oct'41:230

PARIS, TENNESSEE
May'34:116

PARKER. (KENTUCKY)
Apr'38:87

PARKER, W. (KENTUCKY)
Oct'41:223

PARKER'S PRAIRIE, ILLINOIS
Jan'42:22

PARMLY. (NEW YORK)
Apr'32:95

PARRISH, W.
quoted. Oct'38:226

PASLEY, W. (KENTUCKY)
Jan'37C:24

PATHOLOGY
Jan'35:7

PATRIOTISM
Nov'40:254

PATTERSON, C. P.
Jan'37C:24

PATTERSON, NEW JERSEY
Dec'38:288

Paul
Apostacy. Jan'40:13

Paxton.
Letter. Apr'32:95

PAYNE, AUGUST (MISSOURI)
Jul'40:155

PAYNE, B. H. (LOUISIANA)
Oct'41:223

PAYNE, JOHN N. (KENTUCKY)
Dec'39:284
Oct'41:223

Payne, William P. (Kentucky)
Letter. Apr'34:93
Letter. Oct'41:223
Letter. Feb'42:41

PEAKE, H. (KENTUCKY)
Jan'37C:24

PEARCE, J. (KENTUCKY)
Jan'37C:24

PEERS, B. C. (KENTUCKY)
Aug'33:192

PENDLETON, WILLIAM KIMBROUGH
Jan'38:8

PENNSYLVANIA
Feb'32:47   Dec'34:282
Mar'32:71   Mar'35:68
Jun'32:144   Sep(ieOct)'37C:
Aug'32:190   193,199
Jan'33:22   Jan'38:9
Sep'33:212,216   Sep'38:204
Apr'34:94   Dec'38:288

PENNSYLVANIA (cont.)
Jul'39:167
Feb'42:32
Apr'42:82,86
May'42:113,114

PENTECOST
Jun'33:142,143
Mar'41:66

PEOPLE'S MEDICAL SOCIETY
Aug'42:170

Pepper. (Kentucky)
Letter. Jan'33:22

PERIODICALS
   See also
   JOURNALISM
   Names of Individual periodicals
Jan'33:24   Aug'39:189
Oct'33:240   Nov'39:264
Nov'34:264   Apr'40:79,96
Dec'34:281   Jun'40:144
Feb'35:45   Aug'40:192
Nov'35:264   Oct'40:232
Jan'37C:20   Nov'40:256,263
May'37C:99,100   Jun'41:142,144
May'37C:101,117   Jul'41:164
Jun'37C:136,146   Aug'41:192
Jan'38:22   Oct'41:235,237
Feb'38:45,47   Oct'41:238,239
Mar'38:back cover Dec'41:284,285
Aug'38:183,184   Apr'42:87,94
Aug'38:185,186   Jun'42:143

PERKINS, EP.
quoted. Jul'41:149

PERKINS, LUCINDA (KENTUCKY)
Obituary. Oct'41:230

PERSIA (BOON CO.) MISSOURI
Nov'39:263

PERSONAL NAMES
   See
   NAMES, PERSONAL

PETER, SAINT, APOSTLE
Jun'32:143

PETER THE GREAT
Mar'33:60

PETERSBURG (BOON CO.) MISSOURI
Sep(ieOct)'37C:199
Jul'39:153,162
May'40:118
Jul'42:167

PHELPS, PRUDENCE (OHIO)
Oct'42:237

PHILADELPHIA, PENNSYLVANIA
Apr'42:82,86
May'42:113,114

Philip
Reformation.
     no. 1. Mar'35:61
     no. 2. Apr'35:90
     no. 3. Aug'35:172
     no. 4. Sep'35:193

PHILLIPS, U. B. (KENTUCKY)
Jan'37C:23

Philokalos
Presbyterianism an antidote
    against insanity.
    Jul'37C:144

PHILOSOPHY
Jan'32:22
Oct'32:233
Nov'35:253
Dec'39:272
Jul'41:150

PHRENOLOGY
May'42:107

PHYSICS
May'40:108

PHYSIOLOGY
May'42:106

PICKET, A. (OHIO)
Aug'33:192

PIKE, S. (OHIO)
Dec'41:285

PIKADELPHIA, KENTUCKY
Oct'35:239

PINKERTON.
Aug'38:190
Mar'39:70
May'39:119
Aug'40:187
Oct'40:218
Jun'41:140
Oct'42:239

Pinkerton, Lewis Letig
Letter. Jul'39:162
Letter. Sep'39:206
Letter. Oct'40:236

PINKERTON, LEWIS LETIG
Jul'39:153
Mar'40:71
May'40:118
Oct'40:217
Oct'41:223,231,233

Pinkerton, W. (Ohio)
Letter. Apr'41:96

PINKERTON, W. (OHIO)
Jun'42:140

Pinkerton, W., Jr. (Ohio)
Letter. Dec'41:282
Obituary of James Felter.
    Dec'41:283

PINKERTON, WILLIAM (KENTUCKY)
Jul'39:153,162

PIPER, WILLIAM (LOUISIANA)
Jan'37C:24

PITTSBURGH, PENNSYLVANIA

Aug'32:190	Jan'38:9
Jan'33:23	Sep'38:204
Apr'34:94	Dec'38:288
Mar'35:68	Jul'39:167
Sep(ieOct)'37C:	Feb'42:32
199	Apr'42:86

PLYMOUTH, MASSACHUSETTS
Feb'34:47

POEMS
See also
HYMNS
Internal evidence. Feb'32:48
Reflections on the death of a
    Brother, by J. McElroy.
    Aug'32:191
Untitled. Apr'33:85
Untitled, by Graham. Apr'33:90
Untitled, by J. Challen.
    Apr'33:93
Untitled, by J. Challen.
    Oct'33:240
Mother's injunction on presenting
    her son with a Bible.
    Oct'34:240
Shortness of life. Jan'35:20
The Resurrection. Jan'35:20
Untitled (on death). Feb'35:44
Untitled. May'35:112
Untitled. May'35:119
The Olney Kite, by John Newton.
    May'35:120
Lines. Nov'35:263
The Bible. Dec'39:281
Luke VII, by J. C. Feb'40:47
The baptism. Jan'41:24
The baptism of Christ. Mar'41:55
Untitled. Jul'41:168
Paul before Agrippa, by Mrs.
    Sigourney. Oct'41:240
Intemperance, by Mrs. Sigourney.
    Nov'41:264
Right improvement of life, by
    Cowper. Feb'42:48
Thy will be done, by Mary Ann
    Brown. Mar'42:72
A song, by M. Sep'(ieOct)'37C:192

POGGIO OF FLORENCE
quoted. Feb'40:30

Poindexter. (Kentucky)
Letter. Apr'33:94

POLITICS
Jun'35:143

Pomeroy, James
Letter. Mar'40:71
Letter. Nov'40:259

POND, KENTUCKY
Oct(ieSep)'37C:176

PONTIUS PILATE
Nov'39:241

POOL.
Oct'41:233
Jun'42:140

Pool, William F. (Kentucky)
Letter. Aug'42:189

POPE (HEAD OF CATHOLIC CHURCH)
See
CATHOLIC CHURCH. POPE

POPULAR HILL FEMALE SEMINARY
    (KENTUCKY)
Aug'40:192
Oct'40:221

POPLAR RUN, KENTUCKY
May'32:112
May'38:120

PORTER. (NEW YORK)
Jun'34:144

PORTLAND, NEW YORK
Jan'35:21

POWELL. (KENTUCKY)
Aug'40:187
Jun'42:141

Pratt, John, Jr. (New York)
 Progress of the Gospel. Sep'34:216

PRATT, ORSON (MORMON)
 Oct'38:226

PRAYER
 May'40:109
 Aug'41:191
 Jan'42:20

PRCZRIMINSKI, C. R. (KENTUCKY)
 Jan'37C:23

PREACHING
    See also
 PUBLIC SPEAKING
 Jun'32:139
 Jul'32:158
 Mar'33:72
 May'33:117
 Oct'33:237
 Mar'34:63
 Aug'35:169
 Jan'40:13
 Feb'42:34

Presbuteros
    See
 Reneau, Isaac T.

PRESBYTERIANS
 Jul'32:158   Sep'33:216
 Sep'32:206   Jun'37C:133
 Dec'32:282   Jul'37C:144
 Mar'33:60   Aug'38:183
 Apr'33:73   Mar'42:52
 May'33:111

PRESSLY, JOHN T. LECTURES ON THE
    NATURE, SUBJECTS AND MODE OF
    CHRISTIAN BAPTISM
 May'41:106
 Sep'41:193
 Nov'41:252
 Dec'41:275
 Jan'42:9

PREWITT. (MISSOURI)
 Apr'41:95

PREWITT, J. (MISSOURI)
 May'42:118

PRIMITIVE CHRISTIAN (NEW YORK)
 May'37C:101

PRITCHARD. (OHIO)
 Sep'42:215,216

PROFANITY
    See
 SWEARING

PROMISED LAND
 Apr'34:76

PROMISES
    See
 HOPE
 PROPHECIES

PROPHECIES
    See also
 MILLENNIUM
 Apr'32:73   Jan'41:7,13
 Jul'32:150   Feb'41:25,29
 Aug'32:176   Mar'41:49
 Oct'32:224   Apr'41:80
 Apr'34:73   May'41:97,102
 Apr'35:96   Jun'41:121
 Feb'38:39   Oct'41:217
 Mar'39:64   Nov'42:260
 Sep'39:209   Dec'42:278

PROTESTANT AND HERALD
 Nov'40:259

PROTESTANTISM
 Apr'33:73
 Apr'41:96

PROVIDENCE, KENTUCKY
 Oct'40:217
 Nov'40:258
 Oct'42:239

PROVIDENCE AND GOVERNMENT OF GOD
    See also
 KINGDOM OF GOD
 Jul'41:146

PSYCHOLOGY
 May'42:106

PUBLIC SPEAKING
   See also
 PREACHING
 May'40:110
 Jun'40:130

PUGH. (KENTUCKY)
 Dec'41:284

PUNISHMENT
 May'33:115
 Aug'41:188
 Nov'42:246

PURCELL, JOHN BAPTIST. DEBATE WITH
     ALEXANDER CAMPBELL
 Jan'37C:18
 Apr'37C:93
 Jun'37C:136
 Jul'37C:152

Q

QUAKERS
 Apr'33:78
 Sep'33:214
 May'42:112

QUINAN, T. H. (KENTUCKY)
 Aug'33:192

R

R.
 Simplification.
   Feb'34:34
   Mar'34:49

R., A. (Probably Aylett Raines)
 Desultory reflections.
   no. 1. Jan'37C:3
   no. 2. May'37C:111
 Selections. Jan'37C:6
 Letter. Apr'37C:73
 A Bishop reformer.
   Mar'40:57
   Apr'40:90
   no. 3. Jun'40:133
   no. 4. Jun'40:134
 Letter to Alonzo. Jun'41:137

R., C. (Ohio)
 Letter. Sep'39:208

R., O.
 Sects among the Christians.
   Apr'40:73
 Letter. Nov'40:259

R., T.
 Sep'39:209

R., Z.
 Answer to Presbuteros. Oct'41:226

RACE, MICHAEL (KENTUCKY)
 May'42:115

RACE, MOSES (KENTUCKY)
 May'42:115

Radford. (Kentucky)
 Letter. Mar'33:72

RAGLAND, J. (TENNESSEE)
 Jan'37C:24

RAILROADS
 Jun'35:125

Raines, Aylett
   See also
 Articles signed A.R.
 Letter. Jun'32:143
 Letter. Apr'33:95
 To Mr.--- a Universalist.
   May'33:103
 A refutation of the doctrine of
   total hereditary depravity.
   Jun'33:133
 Evangelists. Oct'35:233

RAINES, AYLETT
   Jun'32:143   quoted. Dec'38:273
   Jul'32:166   Mar'40:65
   Jul'35:165   May'40:101
   Apr'38:86   Aug'40:187
   Jun'38:144   Dec'40:284
   Oct'38:225   Jun'41:140
                       Oct'41:223

RAMSEY'S CREEK, MISSOURI
 Sep'33:214

RANDOLPH, INDIANA
 May'38:103

RANDOLPH, MISSOURI
 Sep'33:213

RANDOLPH, OHIO
 Aug'33:190
 Jul'41:166

RAPER, R. H.
 Jan'37C:18

RASH. (KENTUCKY)
 Apr'38:87

RATCLIFFE. (KENTUCKY)
 May'40:101

RAVENNA, OHIO
 Feb'35:42

69

RAY, JOSEPH
Oct'38:235

RAYMOND, G. (MISSISSIPPI)
Jan'37C:24

RAYMOND, RICHARD (KENTUCKY)
Oct'42:239

Read, John (Ohio)
Progress of Reform. Mar'34:71
Letter. Aug'38:192

READYVILLE, TENNESSEE
Jun'32:140

RED OAK (BROWN CO.) OHIO
Jun'32:143
Jul'32:166
Jan'35:23
Oct'35:240
Jan'37C:11

RED RIVER, KENTUCKY
Sep'42:215

RED TOP (BOON CO.) MISSOURI
Nov'39:263

Reed. (Ohio)
Letter. Sep'32:215

Reed, Alex. (Maryland)
Letter. Sep'39:207
Letter. Dec'40:283

REED, ALEXANDER (MARYLAND)
Dec'40:283
quoted. Jan'41:23
Apr'42:74

Reed, J. (Maryland)
Question. Apr'40:96

REED, W. (MISSOURI)
Nov'39:263
May'42:118

REFORMATION--GENERAL
Jan'32:181
Sep'32:184(ie202)

REFORMATION--GENERAL (cont.)
Sep'32:204
Aug'40:171
Jan'41:22

REFORMATION--16TH CENTURY
Jan'32:19
Apr'33:89
Aug'37C:153
Jan'42:7

REFORMATION--19TH CENTURY
Aug'32:181   Jun'35:128
Sep'32:193   Sep'35:214
Nov'32:252   Nov'35:257
Jan'33:1,15   Feb'38:45
Mar'33:50   Apr'38:90
Apr'33:88   May'38:101
May'33:97,100   Jul'38:151
Jun'33:130   Aug'38:180,183
Jul'33:145   Oct'38:238
Sep'33:204,205   Dec'38:268
Oct'33:234   Sep'39:204
Nov'33:253,259   Mar'40:51
Jan'34:14   May'40:97,99
Mar'34:72   Aug'40:171,172,
Jun'34:123   Oct'40:229
Jul'34:153   Dec'40:265
Sep'34:193   Jan'41:3
Dec'34:281   Apr'42:87
Jan'34:4,5   Jun'42:138
Apr'35:87

REGENERATION
    See
BAPTISM
SALVATION

Reid, G. C. (Scotland)
Letter. Nov'40:261

Reid, Walker (Kentucky)
Letter. Feb'32:47

RELIGION
Jan'32:22
Oct'32:233
Feb-Mar'37C:56
Sep(ieOct)'37C:190
Jan'38:6,8

70

RELIGION AND SCIENCE
Jun'42:131

RELIGIONS
Jan'34:3

RELIGIOUS EDUCATION
See
EDUCATION

RELIGIOUS HERALD (BAPTIST)
May'33:118
Aug'33:177
Jun'37C:131

RELIGIOUS LIFE
See
CHRISTIAN LIFE

RELIGIOUS NARRATOR
quoted. Jun'34:123

REMISSION OF SINS
See
SALVATION

Reneau, Isaac T. (Kentucky)
News. Jan'39:24
Letter. Sep'39:207
Letter. Feb'40:46
Letter. Jul'41:163
Letter. Feb'42:40

RENEAU, ISAAC T. (KENTUCKY)
Oct'41:226,231

RENICK, F. W. (OHIO)
Jan'37C:24

REPENTANCE
May'32:100
Aug'33:179
Nov'41:262

Reprover
Letter. Nov'34:260

REPUBLICAN, KENTUCKY
Aug'38:192   Oct'40:218
Jul'39:164   Jun'41:144
Sep'39:205

REPUBLICAN (HARRISON CO.) KENTUCKY
Jun'41:140

Rese, Fred. (Ohio)
Letter. Jul'33:162

RESE, FRED. (OHIO)
Jul'33:163

RESTORATION
See also
REFORMATION--19TH CENTURY
Jan'33:1,15

RESURRECTION
See also
JESUS CHRIST--DEATH AND RESURRECTION
May'33:112
Mar'38:69
Apr'39:83
Jan'40:24
Oct'41:220
Jun'42:127

REVELATION
Apr'35:91
Apr'38:83

REVIVALS
Jun'41:141

Reynolds. (New York)
Letter. Sep'32:214
Letter. Jan'33:22

Reynolds, William P.
Letter. Aug'33:191

RHODE ISLAND
Apr'32:96

RICE. (KENTUCKY)
May'40:101
Jun'41:140
Aug'41:190
Oct'41:223,231
May'42:116
Sep'42:215

RICE, A. (MISSOURI)
Nov'39:263

RICE, N. L.
Nov'40:259

Rice, R. C. (Kentucky)
Letter. Aug'41:189

RICE, R. C. (KENTUCKY)
Jan'42:21
Jun'42:139,140
Aug'42:189

Richardson, Robert
    See also his pseudonyms
    Alumnus
    Discipulus
Extract from modern history of
    the Jews. Oct'32:230
Letter. Jan'33:21
Letter. Apr'34:95
Note. Apr'34:96
Faith cometh by hearing. Feb'35:29
Eternal life. Mar'35:57
Letter. Jul'41:162

RICHARDSON, ROBERT
quoted. Jul'32:167
Jan'38:15
Oct'40:217

RICHFIELD, OHIO
Aug'33:190

RICHLAND (HOWARD CO.) MISSOURI
Nov'39:263

RICHMOND, KENTUCKY
Jun'37C:135
Jul'37C:152
Oct(ieSep)'37C:176
Mar'39:72

RICHMOND, MISSOURI
Jul'40:155

RICHMOND, VIRGINIA
May'32:119
Mar'34:71

RICKETTS. (KENTUCKY)
Jan'35:23
Jan'37C:11

RICKETTS (KENTUCKY) (cont.)
Nov'40:263
Jan'41:23
Mar'41:70
Oct'42:239

Ricketts, R. C.
Progress of the Gospel. Oct'35:
    240
Letter. Apr'37C:96
Conquest of the Gospel. Jul'37C:
    152

RICKETTS, R. C. (KENTUCKY)
Dec'39:284
Dec'40:284

Ricketts, Richard (Kentucky)
Letter. May'38:119

RICKETTS, RICHARD C. (KENTUCKY)
Jun'38:143

RIDDLES
Jun'40:139

RIDER, S.
Jan'38:15

RIGDON, JOHN (ILLINOIS)
Dec'34:280

RIGDON, SIDNEY
Oct'38:226
Dec'38:287
Jul'39:160
Jun'41:133

RISING SUN, INDIANA
Jan'33:24
Jan'35:24
May'38:103

ROACH. (DR.) (INDIANA)
Sep'33:214

Robbins, Samuel (Ohio)
Letter. Jul'39:161

ROBERT. (LOUISIANA)
Feb'42:47

Robert, Louis J. D. (Ohio)
Letter. Jun'34:142

ROBERTS. (KENTUCKY)
Oct'40:220

ROBERTS, J. (KENTUCKY)
Sep'33:213

ROBERTS, JOHN W.
Sep'33:212

ROBERTS, R. R. (METHODIST)
Jun'38:137

Roberts, U. M. (South Carolina)
Progress of the Gospel. Sep'34:212

ROBERTSON, GEORGE (KENTUCKY)
Jan'37C:24

ROBINSON, D. (OHIO)
Sep'39:205

ROBINSON, R. M. (KENTUCKY)
Jan'37C:24

ROCHEPORT (BOON CO.) MISSOURI
Nov'39:263

ROCHESTER, NEW YORK
Sep'32:215

ROCKBRIDGE (BOON CO.) MISSOURI
Nov'39:263

ROCKVILLE, MARYLAND
Sep'39:207

ROGERS.
May'42:102

ROGERS. (KENTUCKY)
Feb'32:30
Mar'32:71
Apr'37C:96
Jul'37C:152
Jun'41:140,144

ROGERS, ELIZA
Obituary. Feb'41:46

ROGERS, ELLEN
Jul'39:164
Obituary. Jul'39:165

ROGERS, I.
Sep'33:213

Rogers, John (Kentucky)
The doctrine of forgiveness
    illustrated and enforced.
    Jan'37C:8
Letter. Jan'37C:10
Letter. Apr'37C:93
Letter. May'37C:117
Obituary of wife. Jul'39:165

ROGERS, JOHN (KENTUCKY)
May'32:110   Sep'39:205
quoted. May'32:112 May'40:102
Sep'33:213   Jul'40:147
Feb'34:48   Aug'40:187
Jan'35:23   Sep'40:214
Jul'35:163   Feb'41:46
Jun'38:143   Oct'41:223
Jul'39:164

ROGERS, SAMUEL (OHIO)
Sep'41:214

Rogers, W. (Kentucky)
Letter. Sep'33:214

ROMAIN. LIFE OF FAITH
Dec'33:270
quoted. Dec'33:271

ROMAN CATHOLIC CHURCH
        See
CATHOLIC CHURCH

ROME, ITALY
Oct'39:228

ROSS, JAMES (INDIANA)
May'34:114

Ross, Samuel
Letter. Mar'35:65

ROSS, SAMUEL
Mar'34:56   Mar'35:65

73

ROWZEE. (PENNSYLVANIA)
Apr'42:82

RUDDEL'S MILLS, KENTUCKY
Dec'41:286

RUDE. (OHIO)
Sep'42:216

RUDOLPH, Z.
Jan'38:15

Rudulph, John, Jr. (Ohio)
Letter. Apr'34:90

RUMBOLD, JAMES (IOWA)
Mar'41:71

Runyan, Asa R. (Kentucky)
Letter. Mar'32:71
Letter. Jun'32:142
Letter. Jan'34:23
Progress of the Gospel. May'34:116
Letter. Jan'35:23
Letter. May'38:119

RUNYAN, ASA R. (KENTUCKY)
Jan'37C:23
Jun'41:127

RUPPEL, M.
Oct'34:240

RUSHVILLE, ILLINOIS
Oct'34:239

Russell. (Louisiana)
Letter. Jun'32:143

RUSSELL, T. A. (KENTUCKY)
Jul'40:156

RUSSELLVILLE, INDIANA
Jun'35:144

RUSSELLVILLE, KENTUCKY
Jan'35:22
Sep'42:215

RUSSIA
Nov'39:250
Jul'41:158
May'42:105

S

S.
  Restoration of the Ancient Gospel.
    Mar'33:50

S., J. P. (Ohio)
  Letter. Dec'42:284

S., W. P.
  Obituary of Lucinda Perkins.
    Oct'41:230

SACKET, MIRAM (OHIO)
  Jan'38:11

Sacket, Myron (Ohio)
  Letter. Feb'32:47
  Progress of Reform. Feb'34:47

SACRED MUSIC
      See also
  HYMNS
  VOCAL MUSIC
  Aug'39:191
  Oct'39:233
  Nov'39:252
  Dec'39:265

ST. LOUIS, MISSOURI
  May'33:111

ST. MARY'S, OHIO
  Nov'40:257

SALEM, MASSACHUSETTS
  Nov'40:256

SALEM, OHIO
  Feb'34:47

SALEM, TENNESSEE
  Sep'42:215

Sallee, Abrm.
  (Address) May'37C:97
  Letter. May'37C:115
  Letter. Sep(ieOct)'37C:199

SALT CREEK (HOWARD CO.) MISSOURI
  Nov'39:263

SALVATION
  Mar'32:60   Jun'38:142
  Jan'33:4,10   Aug'38:185
  May'33:104,119   Oct'38:227
  Oct'33:239   Nov'38:whole
  Jun'34:144   issue (p241)
  Jul'34:151,159   Jul'39:154
  Jan'37C:8   Oct'40:233
  May'37C:107   Dec'40:278
  Jun'37C:122   Aug'41:191
  Jul'37C:144   Oct'41:234
  Apr'38:94   Jan'42:9,20
  May'38:109   Mar'42:52
                     May'42:102,110

SAMUEL, JACOB. THE REMNANT FOUND...
  Mar'42:65

SANDY CREEK, OHIO
  Mar'34:71

SANTA FEE (MONROE CO.) MISSOURI
  Nov'39:263
  Sep'41:214

Sargent, J. (Ohio)
  Item of ecclesaistical intellegence.
      Sep(ieOct)'37C:194

SATAN
      See
  DEVIL

SAUNDERS, JAMES (NEW YORK)
  Jul'38:160

Saunders, John H. (Indiana)
  Letter. Jan'42:24

SAUNDERS, JOHN H. (INDIANA)
  Feb'42:43

SAVANNAH, GEORGIA
  Jun'32:143

SCEPTICISM
  Nov'34:256
  Dec'34:265

SCHMUKER, S. S. (LUTHERAN)
Apr'41:86

SCHOOL OF THE PREACHERS (OHIO)
Jan'38:14
Sep'39:205

SCIENCE
Feb-Mar'37C:25
Jan'42:12
Feb'42:27
Mar'42:49
May'42:106
Jun'42:131

SCIENCE AND RELIGION
    See
RELIGION AND SCIENCE

SCOTLAND
Nov'40:261

SCOTT, E. (KENTUCKY)
Jan'37C:24

Scott, Walter, Sir.
 Sermon.
      Oct'35:224
      Nov'35:244

Scott, Walter
 The volumes of The Evangelist contain
 many articles by Walter Scott.
 Listed below are articles by
 Scott which appear in The
 Christian which was co-edited
 by J. T. Johnson and Scott.
 The state system. Feb-Mar'37C:25
 Letter. May'37C:109
 On union among Christians. Aug'37C:
 153
 Confession. Oct(ieSep)'37C:169
 Dead in sin. Oct(ieSep)'37C:171

SCOTT, WALTER
 Jan'32:18   Jan'37C:23
 Jun'34:144   May'37C:116
 Sep'34:195   Jul'37C:153
 Dec'34:283   Oct(ieSep)'37C:
 Sep'35:204   176,177

SCOTT, WALTER (cont.)
 Sep(ieOct)'37C: Jun'38:139
    199   Oct'38:238
 Jan'38:15   Oct'39:240
 Feb'38:47   Jul'40:157
 May'38:115   Sep'40:201

SCOTT, WALTER. THE GOSPEL RESTORED
 1836 vol.
 Jan'38:23
 Receipts. Mar'38:back cover
 Receipts. May'38:back cover
 Receipts. Jul'38:back cover
 Aug'38:182
 Receipts. Sep'38:back cover
 Aug'39:190
 Jun'40:140

SCOTT, WALTER. TOURS
 Mar'34:54
 May'35:109
 Jun'35:123
 Jan'38:8
 Oct'38:229
 Dec'38:288
 Nov'40:63
 Oct'40:217
 Apr'42:73

Scranton, W. C. (Michigan)
 An affectionate letter. Dec'42:27

Scranton, William A.
 Letter. Aug'33:188

Scratton, B. (New York)
 Letter. Sep'32:215

Scrutator
 Episcopacy and Christianity.
      Nov'34:261

SECRIST. (OHIO)
 Apr'33:95

Secrest, J.
 News. Oct'32:238

SECREST, JOHN
 Dec'38:277

SECRET SOCIETIES
See
FREEMASONS
ODD FELLOWS

SECTARIANISM
Mar'33:63

SECTS
Apr'40:73

SEHON, E. W. (METHODIST)
May'35:108

SELF CULTURE
Aug'41:183

SELF EDUCATION
See
SELF CULTURE

Senex
Discipline
no. 4. Feb'40:34
no. 5. Apr'40:75
no. 6. Aug'40:169
no. 7. Nov'40:252
no. 8. Dec'40:273

SENTINEL AND STAR IN THE WEST
quoted. Mar'33:66

SERGEANT. (OHIO)
Apr'33:95

SERMONS
Oct'35:224
Nov'35:244
Mar'38:60
Nov'41:260

SERVANT AS A NAME
Jan'40'22

SHAFER, I.
Jan'38:15

SHAKER PRAIRIE, INDIANA
Jan'42:22

SHANLEY, WILLIAM (VIRGINIA)
Dec'39:282

SHANNON, JAMES
Sep'40:216
Oct'40:218
Jun'41:127,143,144
Aug'41:190

SHARPSBURG, KENTUCKY
Jan'42:23

SHAW, J. A. (TENNESSEE)
Jan'37C:24

SHAWNEY, KENTUCKY
Jul'37C:151

SHELBYVILLE, KENTUCKY
May'37C:116
Jan'39:24
May'39:119
Oct'40:220
Aug'41:189
May'42:115,116
Jun'42:142

SHELBYVILLE (SHELBY CO.) MISSOURI
Nov'39:264
Sep'41:214

SHEPARD, W. (KENTUCKY)
Jan'37C:24

SHEPHERD. (NEW YORK)
May'35:118
May'37C:101

SHICK. (MRS. PETER) (OHIO)
Obituary. Jul'35:168

SHICK, PETER (OHIO)
Obituary. Jul'35:168

SHIP, C. (MISSISSIPPI)
Jan'37C:24

SHIP, GEORGE (MISSISSIPPI)
Jan'37C:24

SHOCKLEY, ABIGAIL (OHIO)
  Obituary. Jul'35:168

SHOCKLEY, SAMPSON (OHIO)
  Jul'35:168

SHORT. (KENTUCKY)
  Oct'40:219
  Jun'42:141

SHORT, NEWTON
  Apr'37C:93

SHROYER, GEORGE (KENTUCKY)
  Jan'37C:24

SIGNS OF THE TIMES (BOSTON)
  quoted. Jul'41:145,147
  Oct'41:238
  quoted. Dec'42:276

Sigourney, (Mrs. L. H.)
  Paul before Agrippa (poem)
      Oct'41:240
  Intemperance (poem) Nov'41:264

Silas
  Christian decorum.
      Feb'34:40
      Apr'34:85
  The Kingdom of heaven.
      no. 1. May'34:97
      no. 2. Jun'34:121

SILVER CREEK ASSOCIATION (INDIANA)
  Oct'34:235
  Jan'35:18
  Feb'35:39

SIN
      See also
  ORIGINAL SIN
  Jan'32:6
  Aug'33:178
  Jul'35:166
  Oct(ieSep)'37C:171
  Aug'41:192
  Nov'42:246

SLACK, E. (OHIO)
  Aug'33:192

SLAUGHTER, MARTIN
  May'34:115

SLAVERY
  May'33:116   Jun'35:136,138
  Oct'34:234,235   Jun'35:141,144
  Jan'35:17   Jul'35:150
  Feb'35:39   Aug'35:174
  Apr'35:77,80,87   Oct'35:238

Sleigh, W. W.
  Letter. Oct'34:225
  Letter. Nov'34:249

SLEIGH, W. W. (ENGLAND)
  Jun'34:144
  Jul'34:159
  Sep'34:193,204
  Oct'34:228
  Nov'34:251
  Sep'35:213
  quoted. Sep'35:214
  quoted. Oct'35:222

SMALLEY, A.
  Feb'34:47

SMEED. (EPISCOPALIAN) (NEW YORK)
  Mar'34:56

SMITH. (KENTUCKY)
  Jul'32:166
  Jun'37C:136
  Jul'39:164
  Aug'40:187

SMITH, A. (KENTUCKY)
  Dec'39:284

SMITH, C. (KENTUCKY)
  May'40:101

SMITH, C. J. (KENTUCKY)
  Jul'39:164
  Jun'42:139

Smith, Carey (Indiana)
Letter. Feb'35:42
Address to the pamphlet.
   Oct'35:236

SMITH, CAREY (INDIANA)(OHIO)
Jun'34:144
May'38:103

SMITH, CAREY. MYSTERIES EXPLAINED...
Oct'35:236

SMITH, CURTIS J. (KENTUCKY)
Jul'37C:151
Feb'42:45

SMITH, E. A. (KENTUCKY) (ALABAMA)
Jun'34:132
Aug'35:191

SMITH, E. S.
May'37C:101

Smith, Elias
On the new Jerusalem. Aug'34:182

SMITH, EPHRAIM A. (KENTUCKY)
Aug'38:185

SMITH, G. W. H. (KENTUCKY)
Nov'40:257

Smith, John (Kentucky)
A caution to the public. Jan'37C:11

SMITH, JOHN (KENTUCKY)
Feb'32:30   May'38:117
Mar'32:71   Jun'38:143
quoted. May'32:110 Sep'39:205
Jun'32:142   May'40:101
Apr'33:95   Nov'40:257
Feb'34:47   Aug'41:190
Apr'38:86

SMITH, JOSEPH (MORMON LEADER)
Oct'38:226
Jun'41:133
Jul'41:165

SMITH, M. T. (KENTUCKY)
Jan'37C:24

SMITH, PEYTON
Jun'32:140

Smith, Robert
Letter to J. A. Gurley.
   Dec'42:284

Smith, Samuel B.
The recantation of a clergyman.
   Oct'33:229
The logic of Romanism. Sep'35:
   208

SMITH, T. (KENTUCKY)
Feb'32:30
Sep'39:205

SMITH, T. R. (KENTUCKY)
Jan'37C:24

SMITH, THOMAS (KENTUCKY)
Jan'37C:23
Jun'38:144
Jul'39:164
Sep'39:209
May'40:101
Oct'40:218
Feb'42:46
May'42:118

SMITH, THOMAS (MISSOURI)
Apr'41:95
Sep'41:214

SNODGRASS. (KENTUCKY)
Jun'41:144

SOCIETY FOR PROMOTING CHRISTIAN
   KNOWLEDGE
Feb'35:44

SOCIETY OF FRIENDS
   See
   QUAKERS

SOCIOLOGY
Feb-Mar'37C:55

SOCRATES
Dec'39:272

Solomon, J. S. (Kentucky)
Success of the Gospel.
Jan'37C:21

SOMERSET, KENTUCKY
Aug'41:190
Aug'42:189

SOMERSET, PENNSYLVANIA
Dec'34:282
Sep(ieOct)'37C:193

SORROW
See
JOY AND SORROW

SOUL
See
SPIRITUAL BODY

SOULE, JOSHUA (METHODIST)
Jun'38:137

SOUTH CAROLINA
Jun'32:144
Dec'34:282

SOUTH ELKHORN, KENTUCKY
Jul'32:166
Jul'39:164

SOUTHFORK, KENTUCKY
Jun'42:141

Soward, A.
Letter. Jun'32:143

SPAIN
Aug'41:172

Spalding, D. (Kentucky)
Letter. Nov'42:262

SPARKS, ISAAC (OHIO)
May'38:104

SPAULDING, SOLOMON
Jul'39:158

SPENCER, INDIANA
Sep'33:214

SPENCER, KENTUCKY
Aug'42:189

SPIRITUAL BODY
Aug'41:191

SPIRITUAL LIFE
See
CHRISTIAN LIFE

SPIRITUALISM
Nov'42:241

SPRINGFIELD, ILLINOIS
May'33:110
Oct'34:239
Dec'34:279

STAMPING GROUND, KENTUCKY
Sep'33:213
Oct'35:239
Jul'37C:151
Nov'40:258

Stamps. (Mississippi)
Letter. Sep'32:215

STANDIFORD. (KENTUCKY)
Oct'40:220

Standiford, W. (Kentucky)
News. Jan'39:24

STANFORD, KENTUCKY
Jun'42:139

STANWOOD, CAROLINE (KENTUCKY)
Nov'42:262

STATE GOVERNMENTS
Nov'32:264

STEAM SHIPS
Mar'34:54

STEAM SHIPS--ACCIDENTS
Sep'38:209

Steel. (Kentucky)
Letter. Apr'33:95

STEEL. (KENTUCKY)
May'37C:115
Jun'37C:135

STEEL, ELIZABETH (KENTUCKY)
Death. Jun'38:143

Steel, Oliver C. (Kentucky)
Letter. Mar'39:72

STEEL, OLIVER C. (KENTUCKY)
Jun'38:143

Steele, John (Kentucky)
Letter. Oct'33:236

Steele, O. C. (Kentucky)
Conquests of the Gospel. Jul'37C:
152

STEPHENS, J. (KENTUCKY)
Jan'37C:24

STEVENS, J. (EDITOR OF CROSS AND
BAPTIST JOURNAL)
Sep'34:204

STEWARDSHIP
Jan'37C:8

STILES, JOSEPH C. (PRESBYTERIAN)
Jul'37C:144
Oct(ieSep)'37C:168,181
Sep(ieOct)'37C:184

Stockwell, Hugh
The Jews. Dec'33:279

STONE. (KENTUCKY)
Jan'37C:24

STONE, A. (KENTUCKY)
Sep(ieOct)'37C:199

Stone, Barton Warren
Letter. Mar'32:71
Letter. Nov'39:259
The Second coming of Christ.
Jul'42:150

STONE, BARTON WARREN
Feb'32:30   Mar'40:51
Sep'32:215   May'40:101
Jun'33:130   quoted. Jun'40:1
Sep'34:195   Sep'40:216
Dec'34:280,282 Oct'40:224
Jan'37C:12   Jun'41:141
Oct'39:238   Nov'41:248
Nov'39:263.   May'42:102,110
Jan'40:24

STONE MEETING HOUSE, KENTUCKY
Apr'37C:96

STRATTON. (KENTUCKY)
Jul'39:162
May'40:118
Aug'40:187

STREETSBORO, OHIO
Aug'35:192

Striccle, A. S. (Ohio)
News. Jan'39:23

Strickle, E. A. (Ohio)
Letter. Jul'34:165

Strong, William H. (Kentucky)
Questions. Mar'34:62
Question. Jun'34:130
Letter. Oct'34:236
Letter. Jan'35:4

STUTTERD, JOHN (ENGLAND)
Death. Dec'42:283

SULLIVAN. (KENTUCKY)
Jan'37C:24

SULLIVAN. (MISSOURI)
Jan'33:22

SULLIVAN, OHIO
Aug'38:192

Sulmath
Desperate effort--union--no union.
Jun'37C:133

SUNDAY
 Mar'39:51

SUNDAY SCHOOLS
 Apr'37C:92
 Aug'38:191

SUPPORT OF THE CLERGY
 See
 CLERGY SALARIES

SWALLOW, J. (OHIO)
 Apr'41:96

SWEARING
 Jan'32:5
 Aug'38:191

SWEDENBORG
 Dec'40:275

Sweeny, L. S. (Kentucky)
 Success of the Gospel.
 Jan'37C:21

SYMES. (KENTUCKY)
 Oct'40:218

T

T., O.
Dr. Sleigh. Sep'35:213

T., R.
Letter. Jun'40:143

TABERNACLE
Dec'32:279

TAFFE. (OHIO)
Mar'35:72
Jul'35:162

TAFFE, J. (KENTUCKY)
Jun'38:144
May'40:101

TAFFE, JOHN (KENTUCKY)
May'37C:106

Tait, John (Ohio)
Letter. Sep'32:215

TAIT, JOHN
quoted. Dec'38:287

TALENT
May'35:106,107

Tarvor, John (Alabama)
Progress of the Gospel. Sep'34:216

TAYLOR, J. (KENTUCKY)
Jan'37C:24

TAYLOR, J. ORVILLE (NEW YORK)
May'37C:100

TAYLOR, JEREMY
Jan'37C:7

Taylor, Samuel (Indiana)
Progress of the Gospel. May'34:114
Letter. Jul'34:164

Taylor, Thomas (Pennsylvania)
Letter. May'42:114

TAYLOR, THOMAS (PENNSYLVANIA)
Apr'42:81
May'42:113

TEACHERS
Nov'40:90

TEACHING
See also
EDUCATION
Jan'40:13

TECUMSEH (INDIAN CHIEF)
Jun'35:126

TELESCOPES
Oct'40:221

TEMPERANCE
May'33:116
Jul'33:167
Jan'38:22
Aug'38:191
Sep'38:209
Sep'40:212
Jun'41:137
Oct'41:229,234
Jul'42:157

TENNESSEE
Apr'32:95	Aug'38:191
Jun'32:140	Jan'39:24
Aug'32:188,192	May'40:112
Sep'32:213	Nov'40:257
Mar'33:72	Feb'42:47
May'34:116	Sep'42:215

TERRE HAUTE, INDIANA
Jan'42:22
Jun'42:142

THEATER
Jun'34:131

THEOLOGICAL SEMINARIES
Jul'32:168

THEOLOGY
Mar'32:55
Apr'41:88

THOMAS. (NEW YORK)
Apr'34:94

THOMAS, A. (MISSOURI)
May'42:118

Thomas, J. (Pennsylvania)
Letter to Daniel Gano. Nov'33:263

THOMAS, J. E. (BAPTIST) (PENNSYLVANIA)
Aug'41:180

THOMAS, J. E. BAPTISM FOR THE
    REMISSION OF SINS
Aug'41:178,181,186

Thomas, John
Reasons for embracing the Ancient
    Gospel. Nov'32:252
(Note) Jul'41:159

THOMAS, JOHN (VIRGINIA)
Dec'34:282
Feb'35:33
May'37C:100,117
Mar'39:67
Jul'39:157
Jul'41:165
Sep'41:214
Oct'41:237

THOMAS, PORTER (NEW YORK)
Oct'41:233

THOMPSON. (INDIANA)
Sep'33:213

THOMPSON. (KENTUCKY)
May'35:113

THOMPSON, D. (OHIO)
Dec'41:285

THOMPSON, J. (KENTUCKY)
Jan'37C:24

THOMPSON, J. P. (INDIANA)
Dec'33:287

THORNBERRY, W. (KENTUCKY)
Jan'37C:24

TILFORD, T. (KENTUCKY)
Jan'37C:24

Timothy
The office I study in.
    no. 1. Jan'42:11
    no. 2. Feb'42:27
    no. 3. Mar'42:49
    no. 4. May'42:106
    no. 5. Jun'42:131
Identity of Bishop and Elder.
    Jan'42:19

Titus.
A morsel for an infidel. Apr'35:

TOBACCO
May'38:116

TODD, WILLIAM (KENTUCKY)
Jan'37C:24

TOMPKINSVILLE, KENTUCKY
Oct'38:233

TOURS OF WALTER SCOTT
    See
SCOTT, WALTER. TOURS

TRABUE. (KENTUCKY)
Oct'41:223

TREMBLE. (ILLINOIS)
May'34:118

TRIBBLE. (KENTUCKY)
Oct'40:220

TRIMBLE. (INDIANA)
Sep'33:212

TRINITY
Apr'34:88

Trowbridge. (Indiana)
Letter. May'32:119

TROY, MISSOURI
Sep'33:213

TROY, NEW YORK
Jan'33:22

TROY, OHIO
Dec'33:285

TRUMAN. (OHIO)
Oct'41:233

TRUTH
Sep'32:210

TUNKERS
Jul'34:163

TURKEY
Oct'39:226,228   Aug'41:171
Nov'39:249,250   Jul'42:149

TURKEYFOOT, PENNSYLVANIA
Sep(ieOct)'37C:193

Turner, J. M. (Tennessee)
Letter. Nov'40:257

TURPIN, H. H. (KENTUCKY)
Jan'37C:24

TUSCUMBIA, ALABAMA
Jul'35:167
Aug'35:191

TWYMAN, B. (KENTUCKY)
Jan'37C:24

UNION, KENTUCKY
May'32:112
Oct(ieSep)'37C:176

UNION (FAYETTE CO.) KENTUCKY
Sep'40:214

UNION (RANDOLPH CO.) MISSOURI
Nov'39:263

U.S.--DESCRIPTION AND TRAVEL
Apr'42:86

U.S. GOVERNMENT
    See
U.S.--POLITICS AND GOVERNMENT

U.S.--OFFICIALS AND EMPLOYEES
Oct'32:240
Jul'41:167

U.S.--POLITICS AND GOVERNMENT
Jul'38:162
May'41:118

U.S.--SOCIAL POLICY
Jul'38:162

UNIVERSALISM
Mar'33:66
Mar'38:68,72
May'38:105
Aug'38:189,190
Mar'39:68
Aug'39:188
Aug'40:191
Apr'41:92
Jul'41:150
Aug'41:172
Nov'41:247
Sep'42:198
Nov'42:245
Dec'42:276,284

UNIVERSE
Mar'42:61
Nov'42:250,254

UNIVERSITIES
    See
COLLEGES AND UNIVERSITIES

UNIVERSITY OF ALABAMA
Oct(ieSep)'37C:178

USURY
    See
INTEREST AND USURY

V

V
Hints on self-improvment(sic)
    Aug'41:183
The drunkard. Oct'41:229

V., P.
Letter. Feb'38:44

VANCAMP. (MISSOURI)
Jul'40:154

VANCAMP, L. (MISSOURI)
May'42:118

VANCE, JOSEPH (GOVERNOR OF OHIO)
Jan'38:16
Feb'38:36
Mar'38:55
Apr'38:79
Jun'38:121
Sep'38:193

VAN DAKE. (KENTUCKY)
Sep'42:215

VAN DAKE. (OHIO)
Oct'41:230

VANDYKE. (KENTUCKY)
Sep'40:216

VanWinkle, Jesse (Ohio)
Letter. May'39:119

VARDEMAN, J. (EPISCOPALIAN)
Dec'38:275

Vaughn, John P. (Kentucky)
News. Jan'39:24

VAUGHN, JOHN P. (KENTUCKY)
Sep'38:back cover

VERITATIS, AMATOR. BAPTISM DISCUSSED
Review. Aug'32:173

VERMONT
Apr'32:96
Apr'34:90

VERNON, OHIO
Jun'34:144

VERSAILLES, INDIANA
Mar'39:71

VERSAILLES, KENTUCKY
Jul'32:166
Oct'35:239
Jun'37C:133

VIENNE, FRANCE
Nov'39:241

VILEY, J. (KENTUCKY)
Jan'37C:24

VINCENNES, INDIANA
Jan'42:21

VINCENT, T. (KENTUCKY)
Oct'(ieSep)'37C:183

VINT, ANDREWS C.
Jan'37C:11

VINT, NANCY (FARIS)
Jan'37C:11

VIRDEN, J. (KENTUCKY)
May'37C:100

VIRGINIA
Apr'32:95   Dec'34:282
May'32:119   Jan'35:24
Jun'32:144   Jan'38:9
Jan'33:23   May'38:117
Jun'33:139   Mar'39:67
Feb'34:48   Jul'39:161
Mar'34:71   Dec'39:282
Jun'34:144   May'42:117

VOCAL MUSIC
    See also
HYMNS
Aug'38:186

VOCATION
Jul'32:157

87

VOICE - VON

THE VOICE (INDIANA)
Jan'38:22

VON, E. (KENTUCKY)
Jan'37C:24

W

W., M.
Extremes and abuses. Sep'33:204

Wadsworth. (Editor of Louisville
    Berean...)
Universalism. Mar'38:68

WADSWORTH. (EDITOR OF LOUISVILLE
    BEREAN...)
Mar'38:68,72
May'38:105
Aug'38:189,190
Jan'39:24
Mar'39:68

Waite, Daniel (New York)
Letter. May'35:118

WALKER, B. (OHIO)
Apr'33:95

Walker, S. C.
Temporary nature of the material
    system. Jul'40:156

WALKER, T. (OHIO)
Aug'33:192

WALL, S. T. (KENTUCKY)
Jan'37C:24

WALLER, JOHN L. (BAPTIST)
Sep'39:206

Wallis, James (England)
Letter from England. Sep(ieOct)
    '37C:194
Letter. Jan'40:20
Letter. Dec'42:283

WALLIS, JAMES (ENGLAND)
Oct'40:232

WALTER, WILLIAM (KENTUCKY)
Sep'33:214

WARD, ELIJAH (ILLINOIS)
Jan'42:22

WARD, JONATHAN (ILLINOIS)
Jan'42:22

Ward, T. (England)
The starting point. Oct'40:233

WARREN, C. N. (MASSACHUSETTS)
Jan'37C:24

WARREN, OHIO
Oct'33:234
Jan'38:11,14
Oct'49:237

WARRENER. (MISSOURI)
Jul'40:155

WARSAW (GALLATIN CO.) KENTUCKY
Aug'37C:167
Jun'42:141

WASHING OF FEET
    See
FOOT WASHING

WASHINGTON, D.C.
Aug'32:192
Dec'38:288

WASHINGTON, INDIANA
Jan'42:21

WASHINGTON, KENTUCKY
Feb'32:47
Jan'41:23
Jun'42:141

WASHINGTON, PENNSYLVANIA
Jan'33:22

WATERFORD, ENGLAND
Jul'38:160

WATKINS, B.
Jun'34:144

Watkins, B. U. - WHITE, W.

Watkins, B. U.
Universalism philosophy
    no. 1. Jul'41:150
    no. 2. Aug'41:172
    no. 3. Nov'41:247
    no. 4. Dec'41:267
    no. 5. Sep'42:198
    no. 6. Nov'42:245

WATT, JOHN H. (PRESBYTERIAN)
   (KENTUCKY)
Mar'40:69
Jun'40:144

Watts, G. W.
Progress of Reform. May'42:117

WEBSTER, NOAH
Jul'33:165

WEEKLEY. (KENTUCKY)
Jun'41:144
Oct'41:223

WEISIGER, D. (INDIANA)
Jan'37C:24

WELLS. (OHIO)
Apr'33:95

WELLS, M. P. (MISSOURI)
Sep'40:216

WELLSBURG, VIRGINIA
Jun'34:144
Jul'39:161
Dec'39:282

Welly, G. (Ohio)
Letter. Aug'39:191

Welsh. (Virginia)
Letter. Apr'32:95

WESLEYAN MISSIONARY SOCIETY
   (ENGLAND)
Feb'35:44

WEST ALEXANDRIA (PREBLE CO.) OHIO
May'39:119

WESTERN ACADEMICIAN AND JOURNAL
   OF EDUCATION AND SCIENCE
   (OHIO)
May'37C:100

WESTERN CHRISTIAN ADVOCATE
Aug'34:174
Dec'34:278

WESTERN FARMER AND GARDNER
Oct'41:237

WESTERN LUMINARY
Jan'33:4
Mar'33:52
quoted. Jun'33:129

Wharton, William H.
Letter. Jun'34:132
Letter. Jul'35:167

WHARTON, WILLIAM H.
Aug'35:191

WHEELING, VIRGINIA
Jan'33:23

Whip, Peter
Queries. Mar'41:72

WHITACRE, JOHN (OHIO)
Jul'41:166

Whitaker, John
Henry Brown's questions answered
   Jan'42:20

WHITE. (KENTUCKY)
Feb'42:46

WHITE, B.
Jan'37C:24

WHITE, H. H. (KENTUCKY)
Sep'39:205

WHITE, W. (MISSOURI)
May'42:118

WHITE, WILLIAM (MISSOURI)
Nov'39:263,264

WHITE OAK, OHIO
Jan'35:24
May'38:103
Sep'42:215

WHITELOW, H. O.
Jan'38:23

WHITEWATER EVANGELIZING COOPERATION
    (OHIO & INDIANA)
May'38:103

WHITFIELD, R. H. (VIRGINIA)
Jan'37C:22,24

WHITMERS, DAVID
Oct'38:226

WHITMERS, JOHN
Oct'38:226

WICKERSHAM, R. (KENTUCKY)
Jan'37C:24

WICKLIFFE
Jan'32:19

WICKLIFFE, JOHN (EPISCOPAL)
Dec'38:275

WILEY, E. S. (ALABAMA)
Aug'40:190

WILKINSON, W. S. (NEW YORK)
Jan'37C:22,24

WILLIAMS. (OHIO)
Apr'33:95

WILLIAMS, B. (MISSIONARY IN NEW
    ZEALAND)
Sep(ieOct)'37C:198

WILLIAMS, E.
Jan'38:15

Williams, F. (Ohio)
Letter. Feb'35:42

WILLIAMS, G. W. (KENTUCKY)
Jan'37C:23
Sep'40:214
Oct'41:223

Williams, George W. (Kentucky)
Letter. May'38:118

WILLIAMS, J. (LOUISIANA)
Jan'37C:24

WILLIAMS, J. (MISSOURI)
May'42:118

WILLIAMS, JOEL P. (KENTUCKY)
Jul'40:148

WILLIAMS, M. G. (OHIO)
Aug'33:192

WILLIAMS, WILLIAM W. (ALABAMA)
Aug'35:191

WILLIAMS CREEK (INDIANA OR OHIO)
Jul'38:167

WILLIAMSTOWN, KENTUCKY
Sep'33:214
Sep'39:205

WILLIS. (MISSOURI)
Oct'39:238

WILLOW (BRACKEN CO.) KENTUCKY
Jun'42:141

WILLS, M. P. (MISSOURI)
Nov'39:263
Apr'41:95
May'42:118

WILMINGTON (CLINTON CO.) OHIO
Apr'32:95
Apr'33:95
Jun'34:144
Jul'34:165
Mar'35:72
Oct'35:240
May'37C:106
May'38:115
Jan'39:23

WILSON, H. (KENTUCKY)
Jan'37C:24

WILSON, JOSHUA (PRESBYTERIAN)
     (OHIO)
Sep'33:217
Nov'33:241

WILSON'S RUN, KENTUCKY
May'32:112

Winans, Matthias
 Important questions. Apr'33:77
 Letter. Jun'33:141
 Letter. Sep'33:208
 Letter. Oct'33:237
 Letter. Nov'33:255
 Letter. Dec'33:282
 Letter. Mar'34:64
 Letter. Apr'34:96
 Letters. May'34:113
 An argument. Jun'34:130
 Letter. Dec'34:278
 Letter. Apr'35:96
 Letter. May'35:117
 Letter. Jun'35:133
 Letter. Aug'35:190
 Fellowship.
     Jul'37C:137
     Oct(ieSep)'37C:172
 Letter. Apr'38:96
 Letter. Oct'39:237
 Our name. Jan'40:22
 Letter. Sep'40:215
 Letter. Nov'40:258
 Letter. Dec'40:282
 Divine influence. Feb'41:45
 Called and sent preachers.
     Jun'41:126
 Exposition of James, verse 1st,
     chapter 5th. Feb'42:43
 Letter. Feb'42:45
 Letter. Jun'42:140
 Letter. Nov'42:258

WINANS, MATTHIAS
 Feb'34:37
 Mar'34:64
 Jan'39:23
 Apr'40:73
 Jun'41:144

WINCHESTER (CLARKE CO.) KENTUCKY
 Mar'40:65
 Oct'40:221

Winder, D.
 D. Winder and Father Stone.
     May'42:110
 Answer to Bro. Harris.
     Jun'42:123
 Letter. Aug'42:188

WINDHAM (PORTAGE CO.) OHIO
 Apr'38:90

WINN, WILLIS H. (KENTUCKY)
 Jul'40:148

Wirt, Catharine C.
 The last illness of Mr. William
     Wirt. Jan'35:7

WIRT, WILLIAM
 Jan'35:7

WOMAN
 May'38:120
 Mar'40:72
 Jun'40:137
 Feb'41:39
 Jul'41:167
 Jul'42:157

WOMAN--EDUCATION
 Sep'38:211,212

WOOD, T. (ARKANSAS)
 Jul'35:164

WOODFORD, KENTUCKY
 May'42:116

WOODS. (PRESIDENT UNIV. OF ALABAMA)
 Oct(ieSep)'37C:178

WOODSON, W., JR. (MISSOURI)
 Nov'39:263

WOODWARD COLLEGE (CINCINNATI, OHIO)
 Oct'38:235
 Mar'39:54

Woolen, John M. (Indiana)
  Letter. Feb'35:42

WOOLESCRAFT. (METHODIST)
  Sep'39:204

WORD OF GOD
  Jun'38:126

WORSHIP
  Apr'42:80

WORSHIP, ORDER
    See
  ORDER OF WORSHIP

WORTHEN, G. (KENTUCKY)
  Jan'37C:24

WORTHINGTON, L. (KENTUCKY)
  Jan'37C:24

Wright, A. (Missouri)
  Letter. Sep'33:213

WRIGHT, ALLEN (MISSOURI)
  Nov'39:264
  May'42:117

WRIGHT, JOHN C. (JUDGE)
  Jun'32:126

Wright, Joshua (Ohio)
  Letter. Nov'40:257

WYLIE, ANDREW. THE UNION OF CHRIS-
    TIANS FOR THE CONVERSION
    OF THE WORLD
  Feb'35:35
  Mar'35:53

93

XENIA, OHIO
 Jun'42:140

Y., P. G. (Ohio)
 Obituary of James Gaston. Feb'35:47

YANELY. (SISTER) (KENTUCKY)
 Obituary. Jul'37C:152

YARNALL, M. (KENTUCKY)
 Jan'37C:24

YARNALL, MORDECAI (KENTUCKY)
 Oct(ieSep)'37C:183

YEARNSHAW. (NEW YORK)
 Apr'34:94

YORK, NEW YORK
 Apr'32:95

YOUNG. (PENNSYLVANIA)
 Aug'32:190

YOUNG, D. (MISSOURI)
 May'42:118

YOUNG, DUKE (MISSOURI)
 Jul'40:154

Young, Willis W. (Mississippi)
 Letter. Sep'32:214

YOUNG LADIES' MUSEUM (GEORGETOWN,
 KENTUCKY)
 Apr'40:96

YOUNGSTOWN, OHIO
 Feb'32:47

BIBLE
OLD TESTAMENT

NEW TESTAMENT

II PETER I:19-21
 Apr'34:74

REVELATION
 Dec'39:285
 Jul'41:156
 Feb'42:25

REVELATION XIII
 Apr'41:82
 May'41:103

REVELATION XVI:13
 Jan'41:13

REVELATION XXI
 Aug'34:183

ROMANS IV:13
 Apr'32:83

ROMANS V:6
 Mar'35:69

ROMANS VI
 Jul'39:154

ROMANS IX
 Apr'33:85

ROMANS X:9-17
 Nov'41:260

ROMANS XI:26-29
 Apr'34:81

A.

ABUSES, EXTREMES AND
Sep'33:204

ACTS 17
Oct'42:226

ADDRESS TO CONGREGATIONS IN INDIANA
Jul'42:162

ADDRESS TO THOSE WHO HAVE OBEYED THE
ANCIENT GOSPEL
Jan'34:1

ADVERTISEMENT
Oct'33:240
Oct'39:240
Jun'42:144

ADVICE
Jul'41:167

ADVOCATE, APOSTOLIC
Jun'34:128

ADVOCATE, BIBLE
Jun'42:143

ADVOCATE FOR THE TESTIMONY OF GOD
May'37:100
Jul'39:157

ADVOCATE, THE GOSPEL
Nov'34:264
Feb'35:45
Dec'41:285

AFFLICTION
Aug'41:191

AGENTS
Aug'34:192

AGENTS, NEW
Sep'38:217
Feb'40:47

AGRIPPA, PAUL BEFORE
Oct'41:240

ALDEN, CHARLES O.
Letter. May'40:118

ALGEBRA-INDUCTIVE METHOD BY JOHN HARVEY
Feb'41:48

ALLEGORISTS, THE LETTER MEN AND
Jul'35:153

ALLEN, THOMAS M.
Letter. Sep'33:213
Oct'39:238
Nov'39:263
Jul'40:154
Sep'40:216
Apr'41:95
Sep'41:214
Oct'41:230
May'42:117

ALLIN, PHILIP T.
Letter. Jul'40:146

AMEND, WILLIAM
Letter. Jul'33:160

AMERICAN BOARD OF FOREIGN MISSIONS
May'33:120

ANABAPTISM
May'40:112

ANCIENT GOSPEL
Jul'33:167

ANCIENT GOSPEL, OBJECTIONS TO THE
Apr'32:85

ANCIENT GOSPEL, PROFESSED RESTORERS OF
Jun'34:122
Jul'34:153

ANCIENT GOSPEL, RESTORATION OF THE
Oct'32:217
Nov'32:252
Jan'33:1,15
Mar'33:50
Apr'33:88
May'33:97
Jul'33:160

B.

BEGG, WILLIAM
   Letter. Sep'39:205
           Jan'42:21
           Jun'42:142

BENEDICT, H. T. N.
   Letter. Apr'37:93

BENEVOLENT WORK
   Mar'40:72

BENNETT, DR.
   Mar'35:64

BENSON, W.
   Letter. Aug'41:180

BENTLEY, ADAMSON
   Letter. Dec'38:273
           Sep'39:205
           May'40:113,117

BEREAN, THE
   Aug'38:186

BETHLEHEM, A SCENE IN
   Mar'41:68

BIBLE
   Jan'32:1
   Oct'34:240
   May'39:107
   Dec'39:281
   Jan'40:22
   May'40:110
   Jun'40:121
   Jul'42:155

BIBLE ADVOCATE
   Jun'42:143

BIBLE CIRCULATION OF THE
   Oct'42:240

BIBLE, MORMON
   Jul'39:158
   Jan'41:17
   Feb'41:42
   Mar'41:62
   May'41:111
   Jun'41:132

BIBLE, STUDY ON, IN COMMON SCHOOLS
   Sep'38:200,201

BIBLICAL CHRONOLOGY
   Sep'42:193
   Nov'42:253

BISHOP AND ELDER, IDENTITY OF
   Jan'42:19

BISHOP REFORMER, A
   Mar'40:57
   Apr'40:90
   Jun'40:133,134

BLAZEN, W.
   Letter. Sep'39:208

BLOOD OF JESUS CHRIST
   May'38:109

BODENHAMER, W.
   Letter. Oct'33:234

BONAPART'S OPINION OF CHRIST
   May'42:109

BOOKS, SCHOOL
   Feb'41:47

BOON, H. L.
   Letter. May'42:118

BOONE AND CAMPBELL COUNTIES, KENTUCKY
   Sep'39:204

BOOTWRIGHT, WILLIAM
   Letter. May'32:119
           Mar'34:71

BOSWORTH, M.
   Letter. Feb'34:47

BRETHREN, TO THE
   Mar'39:62

BROTHER, DEAR
   May'34:119

BROWN, JOHN
   Obituary. Jul'35:168

BROWN, HENRY
   Letter. Oct'41:227
           Feb'42:46

BROWN, R. T.
  Letter. May'38:103

BROWN'S, HENRY, QUESTIONS ANSWERED
  Jan'42:20

BRUCE, R. C.
  Letter. May'38:117

BRYANT, JOSEPH
  Letter. Mar'35:68

BUCHANAN, N.
  Letter. Sep'37:195

BUCHANAN, W. P.
  Letter. Aug'41:180

BUCKLEY, W. C.
  Letter. Aug'41:189
          Jun'42:142

BURLINGTON, KENTUCKY, MEETING AT
  Jul'39:167

BURNAM, H.
  Letter. Sep'33:214

BURNETT, DAVID S.
  Letter. Oct'32:239
          Dec'33:281
          Jul'34:159,160
          Aug'34:174
          May'37:106

BURTON, G. W.
  Letter. Oct'32:238

BURTON, J. J.
  Letter. Mar'34:72
          Jul'34:163
          May'38:117

BUTLER, CHANCEY
  Letter. Sep'35:216

BUTLER, JAMES A.
  Letter. Oct'32:238
          Dec'33:283
          Nov'34:260
          Aug'35:191
          Jan'39:24

BUTLER, W.
  Letter. Aug'41:180

C.

CAESAR VS THE CHRISTIAN
Sep'38:197

CALAHAN, J.
Letter. Dec'39:284

CALCULATIONS OF WILLIAM MILLER
Jun'41:144
Jul'41:145
Aug'41:176

CALLED AND SENT PREACHERS
Jun'41:126

CALVINISM
Apr'37:83
Jun'38:139

CAMPBELL, ALEXANDER
Jan'34:20
Jan'41:23

CAMPBELL, ALEXANDER
Letter. Sep'33:212
Oct'33:233
Jul'34:167
Oct'39:237
Nov'39:259

CAMPBELL, A., JOHN THOMAS, DIFFICULTIES
BETWEEN
Mar'39:67

CAMPBELL, DAVID, GREAT CONCESSION OF
Sep'42:205

CAMPBELL, GEORGE
Letter. May'38:105
Oct'41:231
Sep'42:215

CAMPBELL, MARGARET
Obituary. Nov'32:263

CAMPBELL-PURCELL DEBATE ON ROMAN CATHOL-
ICISM
Jan'37:18
Jun'37:136
Jul'37:152

CANON OF INTERPRETATION
Nov'42:260

CARMAN, WILLIAM
Letter. Mar'33:72
Mar'34:71
Feb'35:42
Dec'40:282

CARTHAGE, OHIO
Oct'33:240
Nov'40:263

CARTHAGE, OHIO, CHURCH IN
Dec'40:276

CARTHAGE, MEETING AT
Oct'33:238
Oct'35:240
Aug'40:192
Sep'41:216

CASE, A
Jun'35:135,136

CATECHISM, ASSEMBLY'S
Sep'32:206
Dec'32:282

CATHOLICISM
Aug'35:182
Dec'35:278

CATHOLICS, CONVERSION OF THE WORLD BY
THE ROMAN
Oct'42:235

CAUTION TO THE PUBLIC
Jan'37:11

CHALLEN, JAMES
Letter. May'34:117,119
Jul'38:167
Feb'40:41
Sep'41:216
Aug'42:188

CHAMBERS, URIEL B.
Letter. Sep'34:202

CHARACTER, CHURCH
Aug'33:169
Nov'33:259

CHARACTER, FORCE OF
Sep'40:193

COMBS, M.
  Letter. Sep'33:214
           Jun'35:135

COMES, JOB
  Letter. Jan'41:23

COMING OF CHRIST
  Jul'41:147

COMINGS, A. C.
  Letter. Nov'40:264

COMMENTARY
  Oct'32:226

COMMENTARY ON ISAIAH 18
  Oct'39:228

COMMITTING THE ORACLES, ON
  Jul'33:154
  Aug'33:171

COMMON SCHOOL ADVOCATE
  May'37:100,101

COMMON SCHOOL ASSISTANT
  May'37:100

CONCERT SACRED
  Sep'38:214

CONCLUSION
  Dec'34:281

CONFESSION
  Nov'32:249
  Oct'37:169
  May'38:119
  Apr'39:73

CONFESSION, AN INTERESTING
  May'40:107

WISE, MR.
  Mar'39:71

CONQUESTS OF THE GOSPEL
  May'37:116
  Jun'37:135
  Jul'37:151

CONSCIENCE, PERFECTION OF THE
  Jul'39:145

CONSIDERATION
  Dec'39:279

CONSTITUTION OF THE PEOPLE'S MEDICAL
SOCIETY
  Aug'42:170

CONTEMPLATION OF THE STARRY HEAVENS
  Mar'42:61

CONTENTMENT
  Dec'39:280

CONTROVERSY BETWEEN A CATHOLIC AND A
PROTESTANT
  Apr'33:73

CONVENT, SIX MONTHS IN A
  Jul'35:145
  Aug'35:178

CONVERSATION
  Dec'39:280

CONVERSATION BETWEEN A CHRISTIAN AND T
JEWS
  May'40:105

CONVERSATION BETWEEN WALTER SCOTT AND
MR. STEVENS
  Sep'34:204

CONVERSATION ON THE MILLENNIUM
  Feb'32:44
  Apr'32:73
  Jun'32:121

CONVERSATION WITH A JEW
  Oct'42:231

CONVERSION
  Jun'40:135
  Jul'40:150

CONVERSION OF JEWS
  Apr'40:84

CONVERSION OF THE WORLD BY ROMAN CATHO-
LICS
  Oct'42:235

CONVERSION, POPULAR
  Dec'33:270

CONVERSION, THE CHURCH—JESUS
  May'32:102

CONVERSIONS
  May'38:116
  Oct'38:232

COONS, Z.
  Letter. Sep'39:207

COOPERS RUN, KENTUCKY, MEETING AT
  Jun'41:140

COPE, J.
  Letter. Jan'39:23

CORRECTIONS
  Jan'35:24
  Sep'39:215,216
  Sep'42:205

CORRESPONDANCE
  Apr'32:95
  Jun'32:142
  Jul'32:166
  Aug'32:188
  Sep'32:213
  Oct'32:238
  Jan'33:21
  Mar'33:72
  Apr'33:94
  Aug'33:188
  Sep'33:211
  Oct'33:233
  Nov'33:255,261
  Dec'33:281
  Jan'34:20
  Mar'34:64
  Aug'34:186
  Dec'34:278
  Jan'35:22
  Feb'35:42
  Sep'37:185

CORRESPONDANCE—CHRISTIAN CHURCHES IN
AMERICA AND EUROPE
  Jul'38:151

COURSE, OUR
  Nov'40:241

COVENANTS, THE
  Aug'39:169

CRAFT, JOHN B.
  Letter. Feb'34:48

CRAWFORD, WILLIAM
  Letter. Dec'40:285
          Sep'41:215

CREATH, JACOB, JR.
  Letter. Aug'35:189
          May'38:118
          Jul'41:166

CREATH, JACOB, SEN.
  Letter. Mar'32:71

CREATION
  Jul'42:160

CRIHFIELD, A.
  Letter. Oct'38:227
          Oct'41:230

CRISIS, THE
  Nov'35:272

CRITICISM
  May'32:117
  Aug'32:203

CROSS, THE PUNISHMENT OF THE
  Jul'40:163

CYRUS, H. A.
  Letter. Oct'34:239

D.

DIRECT OPERATION OF THE HOLY SPIRIT
May'37:97

DISCIPLE
May'37:100

DISCIPLE EXAMINED, ARGUMENTS FOR
Mar'40:60

DISCIPLINE
Mar'38:72
Jun'38:132
Sep'38:214
Jan'40:8,10,12,18
Feb'40:34
Apr'40:75
Aug'40:169
Nov'40:252
Dec'40:273

DISCIPLINE, FAMILY
Oct'38:223
Mar'39:58

DISCOURSE ON EPHESIANS 3:1
May'37:97

DISCOURSE ON THE HOLY SPIRIT
Feb'33:26

DISPENSATIONS
Apr'32:92
Oct'35:224

DISPUTATION
Dec'39:281

DIVINE CORRECTION
Aug'41:188

DIVINE INFLUENCE
Feb'41:45

DIVINE REVELATION
Apr'38:83

DIVINITY OF CHRIST
Jul'41:149

DIVISION, RELIGIOUS
May'37:101

DONOGH, R. P.
Letter. Mar'39:72

DOWLING, JACKSON
Letter. May'34:115
Feb'35:42

DOWLING, WILLIAM
Letter. Apr'33:95

DR. BEECHER
Jun'32:124
Jul'32:165

DR. FIELD
Jun'35:138

DR. SLEIGH
Sep'35:213

DRINKING
Sep'40:212

DRUNKARD
Oct'41:229

DRUNKENNESS
Jul'33:167

DUELING
May'42:112

DUNGAN, FRANCIS
Letter. Apr'42:93

DUNKESON, WASHINGTON
Letter. Sep'33:214

DUNN, J. H.
Letter. Feb'42:47

DUNNING, S. C.
Letter. Jun'32:143
Apr'33:94
Jun'40:142
Jul'41:166

DUVAL, JOHN
Letter. Jun'33:139

DUVAL'S PAMPHLET
Aug'33:177

E.

E., D.
Letter. Aug'35:186

E., S. A.
Letter. Feb'35:43

EAST AND WEST, THE
Mar'42:86

EATON, W. W.
Letter. Oct'41:233

ECCLESIASTICAL HISTORY
Sep'37:195

ECCLESIASTICAL INTELLIGENCE
Sep'37:193

ECCLESIASTICAL REGISTER
Apr'32:96
Jun'32:144
Aug'32:192

EDAX
Letter. Aug'40:189

EDUCATION
Mar'39:52
May'39:100,106,108

EDUCATION, FEMALE
Sep'38:211

EDUCATION, THEORY OF TRUE
Jan'38:16
Feb'38:36
Mar'38:55
Apr'38:79
Jun'38:121
Sep'38:193

ELDER, IDENTITY OF BISHOP AND
Jan'42:19

ELDERS
Mar'41:72

ELECTION
Apr'33:85
May'37:107

ELLEY, GEORGE W.
Letter. Feb'32:30
Jul'32:166

ELLIS, JOHN G.
Letter. Sep'37:199
Jul'39:161
Sep'39:207
Sep'40:216
Apr'41:96
Oct'41:232
Sep'42:216

EMANCIPATION, A PLAN OF
Apr'35:80

EMMONS, F. W.
Letter. Mar'35:70
Dec'40:282

ENCELL, JOHN
Letter. Mar'34:71

ENGINEERS, SCHOOL FOR CIVIL
Mar'35:72

ENGLAND, THE CHURCH IN
Sep'39:201

ENGLISH SCHOOL, CLASSIC
Jan'39:20
Mar'39:52
May'39:100

EPHESIANS 3:1, A DISCOURSE ON
May'37:97

EPHESUS AND ITS VICINITY
Apr'40:93

EPISCOPACY AND CHRISTIANITY
Nov'34:261

EPISCOPAL
Jan'35:17

EPISTLE OF PAULUS
Mar'33:63

EPISTOLARY CORRESPONDANCE BETWEEN
CHRISTIAN CHURCHES
Jul'38:151

ERRETT, R & I
  Letter. Sep'38:214

ETERNAL LIFE
  Mar'32:52
  Mar'35:57
  Feb'39:25
  Mar'39:61,70

EUROPE, THE KINGDOMS OF
  Aug'42:171

EUROPEAN POWERS
  Apr'33:96

EUSEBIUS
  Letter. Jul'35:153

EVANGELICAL REVIEW
  May'37:100

EVANGELIST, FOR THE
  Sep'32:202,204,210,211
  Dec'32:277
  Apr'33:93
  Oct'33:240

EVANGELIST, IMPROVEMENT OF THE
  Nov'39:264

EVANGELIST IN THE FIELD, ANOTHER
  Mar'35:72

EVANGELIST, ON THE OFFICE OF THE
  Apr'35:93

EVANGELIST, PLEA FOR THE
  Apr'42:94

EVANGELIST, THE
  Mar'40:72
  Feb'41:48

EVANGELISTS
  Jul'35:162,165
  Oct'35:233
  Aug'38:174,189
  Mar'40:62

EVANGELISTS, PRIMITIVE
  Apr'37:73

EVANS, ABRAHAM K.
  Letter. Sep'39:216

EVENTS OF 1823 AND 1827
  Dec'38:266

EVIDENCES OF RELIGION
  Aug'39:192

EWING, JANE C.
  Obituary. Jul'34:166

EXCLUSION
  Sep'35:216

EXCURSION TO VIRGINIA
  Mar'34:54,58

EXECUTIVE GOVERNMENT
  Oct'32:240

EXHORTATION
  Nov'32:249
  Apr'38:77

EXISTENCE OF DEITY
  Jul'37:148
  Sep'37:184

EXPERIENCE, RELIGIOUS
  Mar'41:65

EXPERIMENT OF DR. HUNTER
  Oct'41:234

EXPOSITION OF 1 CORINTHIANS 15:29
  Jun'42:127

EXPOSITION OF JAMES 5:1
  Feb'42:43

EXTRACT OF LETTER TO MAHONING ASSOCIATIO
OF 1830
  Feb'32:40

EXTRAORDINARY PHENOMENON
  Nov'42:250

EXTREMES AND ABUSES
  Sep'33:204

F., B.
  Letter. Sep'39:208

FAITH
  May'38:111
  Oct'41:222

FAITH ACCORDING TO SWEDENBORG
  Dec'40:275

FAITH, A DEFINITION IN FACT
  Mar'32:50
  Apr'32:84

FAITH AND ORDER
  Apr'42:88

FAITH COMETH BY HEARING
  Feb'35:29

FAITH, NATURE AND CAUSES OF, CONSIDERED
  Jul'33:168
  Aug'33:182

FAITH OF THE GOSPEL
  Dec'42:273

FAITH, PROPOGATION OF THE
  Sep'42:207

FALL, PHILIP S.
  Letter. Sep'32:213
           Jan'37:14

FALSIFICATION OF THE SCRIPTURES
  Jul'33:164

FAMILIES, NON-WORSHIP
  Apr'40:89

FAMILY CHARACTER
  Sep'33:202

FAMILY DISCIPLINE
  Oct'38:223
  Mar'39:58

FAMILY LIBRARY
  Dec'41:284

FARQUAR, BROTHER
  Letter. Apr'32:95

FARQUHARSON, CHARLES
  Letter. Oct'41:232

FATHERS, PROMISES MADE UNTO THE
  Apr'34:73

FELLOWSHIP
  Jul'37:137
  Oct'37:172
  Mar'38:59,63

FELLOWSHIP OF THE FIRST CHRISTIAN CO
GREGATIONS
  Mar'38:60
  May'38:97

FELTER, JAMES
  Obituary. Dec'41:283

FEMALE ACADEMY, HYGIEA
  Oct'39:240
  Aug'40:192
  Oct'41:236
  Jun'42:142
  Nov'42:163

FEMALE COLLEGIATE INSTITUTE AT GEORG
TOWN
  May'38:120
  Oct'38:233
  Jun'40:137
  Sep'40:206
  Aug'42:186
  Nov'42:262

FEMALE EDUCATION
  Sep'38:211

FEMALE SEMINARY
  Sep'37:199

FEMALE SEMINARY AT POPLAR HILL
  Aug'40:192

FEMALES, DRESS OF
  Jul'42:157

FERGUSON'S ASTRONOMY, EXTRACT FROM
  Nov'42:254

FIELD, NATHANIEL
  Letter. Oct'34:233
           Jan'35:17
           Apr'35:77
           Jun'35:138
           Dec'42:283

FIGURES
  Nov'32:247

FINANCE
  Sep'35:212

FIRMNESS
  Dec'39:280

FLEMING. L. J.
  Letter. Sep'33:212

FLINN, L.
  Letter. Sep'33:213

FORBEARANCE
  Jun'38:128
  Jul'38:145

FOREIGN MISSIONS, AMERICAN BOARD OF
  May'33:120

FOREIGNERS, NATURALIZATION LAWS
  Aug'35:183

FOREKNOWLEDGE AND FOREORDINATION
  Feb'38:39
  Mar'39:64

FORGIVENESS
  Dec'39:280

FORGIVENESS AND HOLINESS
  Aug'41:191

FORGIVENESS ILLUSTRATED
  Jan'37:8

FORMATION OF CHRISTIAN CHARACTER
  May'32:97
  Jun'32:126
  Jul'32:153
  Nov'32:245
  Dec'32:265,269

FORMATION OF FAMILY CHARACTER
  Jun'33:121
  Jul'33:149
  Sep'33:202

FORRARD, A.
  Letter. Apr'32:95

FORRESTER, ROBERT
  Letter. Apr'34:94

FORSAKING THE ASSEMBLY
  Jan'40:13

FOURTH OF JULY
  Sep'38:207

GANO, DANIEL
  Letter. Jul'33:163
           Nov'33:263

GANO, JOHN ALLEN
  Letter. Oct'38:232
           Jan'39:23
           Sep'40:213
           May'41:119
           Jun'41:144
           Dec'41:286
           May'42:117

GASTON, JOSEPH
  Obituary. Feb'35:46

GENERAL ASSEMBLY
  Jul'32:158

GENESIS, LESSONS ON
  Feb'38:29

GENIUS AND TALENT
  May'35:107

GENIUS OF CHRISTIANITY
  Jul'41:164

GENUINNESS OF THE SCRIPTURES
  Aug'38:181

GEOLOGISTS, A NUT FOR
  Aug'40:188

GEORGETOWN, KENTUCKY, FEMALE INSTITUTE
  May'38:120
  Oct'38:233
  Jun'40:137
  Aug'42:186
  Nov'42:262

GLASPELL, JAMES
  Letter. Mar'41:71

GLEN, NATHANIEL E.
  Letter. Apr'32:95

GLOBE, THE
  Jun'40:131

GLORY, DEGREES OF
  Oct'41:233

GOD IS LOVE
  Aug'37:167

GOD, THE OMNIPOTENCE OF
  May'40:108

GOD, OUR ACCEPTANCE WITH
  Jul'40:153

GOD, THE DEEP THINGS OF
  Jun'40:132

GOD'S LAW
  Apr'39:96

GOD'S OMNIPRESENCE
  May'40:109

GOD'S PERFECTIONS
  Oct'41:227

GOD'S WORD, THE POWER OF
  Jun'38:126

GORDON, D.
  Letter. Jan'34:24
           Feb'34:46

GORDON, J. W.
  Letter. Mar'39:71
           May'42:120

GOSNEY, F.
  Letter. Sep'32:213
           Apr'34:94
           Jul'35:167

GOSPEL
  Jun'33:144

GOSPEL, AN ADDRESS TO THE PROFESSED
RESTORERS OF THE ANCIENT
  Jun'34:122
  Jul'34:153

GOSPEL, AN ADDRESS TO THOSE WHO HAVE
OBEYED THE ANCIENT
  Jan'34:1

GOSPEL ADVOCATE
  Nov'34:264
  Feb'35:45
  Dec'41:285

GOSPEL, CHURCH ORDER AND MINISTRY
  Sep'35:196

GOSPEL, CONQUESTS OF THE
  May'37:116
  Jun'37:135
  Jul'37:151

GOSPEL, FAITH OF THE
  Dec'42:273

GOSPEL, HOPE OF THE
  May'42:98

GOSPEL, PROGRESS OF THE
  May'34:114
  Sep'34:212
  Sep'35:215
  Oct'35:239
  May'42:115

GOSPEL RESTORED, THE
  Jan'38:23
  Aug'38:182
  Oct'38:217

GOSPEL, SUCCESS OF THE
  Jan'37:20
  Apr'37:93
  Oct'37:176
  Jan'38:24

GOSPEL, THOUGHT ON THE RICHES OF THE
  Dec'38:265

GOVERNMENT
  May'41:118

GOVERNMENT, EXECUTIVE
  Nov'32:240

GOVERNORS OF STATES
  Sep'32:216

GRACE, GROWTH IN
  Aug'41:192

GRAFTON, SAMUEL
  Letter. Apr'33:94

Feb'34:48
Jan'35:24
Jul'39:161
Dec'39:282

GREATEST MAN, THE
  Jul'40:156

GREENWELL, GEORGE
  Letter. Dec'42:282

GRIMKE'S ADDRESS
  Feb'32:37
  Mar'32:67
  Jun'32:136
  Aug'32:185

GUIZOTT ON CIVILIZATION
  Nov'39:253

HENRY, JOHN
  Letter. Mar'39:71

HENSHALL, JAMES
  Letter. Jun'42:129

HERALD, THE, VS BACON COLLEGE
  Jun'37:131

HERETIC DETECTOR, THE
  May'37:100
  Jul'37:146
  Apr'38:91
  Aug'38:185

HERODIANS, THE
  Sep'35:202

HIGHLAND COUNTRY, A VISIT TO
  Oct'38:229

HIGH WAY OF HOLINESS
  Aug'38:184

HILL, MILTON H.
  Letter. May'39:113

HIMES, JOSHUA W.
  Letter. Mar'35:64

HISTORICAL SKETCH OF MEETING AT
NORTH MIDDLETOWN, KENTUCKY
  Apr'38:85

HIXON, NATHAN
  Letter. Mar'33:66

HOLINESS, FORGIVENESS AND
  Aug'41:191

HOLINESS, HIGHWAY OF
  Aug'38:184

HOLMES, ERASTUS
  Letter. Jul'39:162

HOLTON, J. H.
  Letter. Oct'33:236

HOLTON, JOHN M.
  Letter. Jun'42:141
         Jul'42:167

HOLY SPIRIT
  Sep'33:197
  Mar'34:68
  Aug'34:175,177,178

HOLY SPIRIT AND REMISSION, THE
  Jan'33:2

HOLY SPIRIT, DIRECT OPERATION
OF THE
  May'37:97

HOLY SPIRIT, THE MISSION OF THE
  Feb'33:33

HONESTY
  Jun'42:192

HOPE
  Apr'37:78

HOPE, THE OBJECT OF
  Oct'40:235

HOPE OF THE GOSPEL, THE
  May'42:98

HOPE, THE REASON FOR OUR
  Feb'38:42

HOPKINS, JOHN M.
  Letter. Jan'33:22

HOWARD, BENJAMIN
  Letter, Oct'35:220

HOWARD, JOHN R.
  Letter. May'34:116

HOWARD, JOHN. S.
  Letter. May'34:118

HUBBARD, E. B.
  Letter. Feb'40:45

HUGHES, J. H.
  Letter. Sep'33:214

HUME'S ARGUMENT AGAINST MIRACLES
  Jun'39:121

HUNDLEY, J. S.
  Letter. May'40:113

HUSBANDS, TO
   Oct'40:227

HYGIEA FEMALE ACADEMY
   Oct'39:240
   Aug'40:192
   Oct'41:236
   Jun'42:142
   Nov'42:163

HYMN
   Nov'34:263
   Mar'35:71

HYMN BOOK
   Aug'39:191
   Sep'39:216
   Oct'39:239
   Dec'39:276

I.

JAMES 5:1, AN EXPOSITION OF
Feb'42:43

JAMESON, ELIZABETH M.
Obituary. Jul'41:167

JAMESON, LOVE H.
Letter. Jan'35:24
Aug'35:189
May'37:117
Jul'38:167
Aug'38:191
Oct'40:238

JAPHET, REMAINS OF
Jun'32:132

JEROME, DEATH OF
Feb'40:30

JERUSALEM
Aug'41:171

JERUSALEM, NEW
Aug'34:182
Dec'34:271

JERUSALEM, ROME AND
Oct'39:228
Aug'41:172

JESUS
Jan'33:17
Jul'40:152

JEW, CONVERSATION WITH A
Oct'42:231

JEWISH SECTS
Sep'35:200

JEWS
Jul'32:150
Aug'32:176
Oct'32:223
Dec'33:279

JEWS AT DAMASCUS
Sep'40:212

JEWS, CONVERSION OF, IN PALESTINE
Apr'40:84

JEWS, DAGHISTAN, OR LOST TRIBES OF
ISRAEL
Mar'42:65

JEWS' LOVE OF JUDEA
Sep'40:211

JEWS, MODERN HISTORY OF THE
Oct'32:230

JEWS, PERSECUTION OF THE
Oct'40:235

JEWS, PROPOSITIONS TO THE
May'42:105

JEWS, PROSPECTS OF THE
May'40:112

JEWS, RESTORATION OF THE
Jul'32:150
Aug'32:176
Oct'32:223
Jan'33:13
Sep'40:209

JEWS, RETURN OF THE
Oct'39:226,228
Nov'39:249

JOHN DUVAL'S PAMPHLET
Aug'33:177

JOHNSON, ILLNESS OF JOHN T.
Mar'39:72

JOHNSON, JOHN T.
Letter. Feb'34:47
Oct'35:239
Jan'37:20
Apr'37:96
May'37:101,106,109,115,
116,117
Jun'37:136
Jul'37:151
Aug'37:167
Oct'37:176,177,178

Sep'37:185,188,189,
190,199
Jan'38:24
May'38:117
Aug'38:192
Sep'38:211
Oct'38:233
Dec'38:266
Jan'39:23
Mar'39:70
May'39:119
Jul'39:162,163,164
Sep'39:205,209
Oct'39:236
Dec'39:284
Mar'40:69
Apr'40:95
May'40:114
Jun'40:142
Aug'40:191
Sep'40:215
Nov'40:258
Dec'40:284
Jan'41:23
Mar'41:70
Jun'41:140
Aug'41:190
Oct'41:231
Jan'42:23
Feb'42:45
Mar'42:116
Jun'42:139,140
Oct'42:239

JOHNSON, THOMAS C.
  Letter. Sep'33:214
          Mar'35:69

JOHNSON, T. F.
  Letter. Jan'37:12

JONES, JOHN T.
  Letter. May'33:109
          Dec'34:279
          Jul'35:166

JOURDAN, W. D.
  Letter. Jun'37:135,136
          Dec'41:286
          Jul'42:152

JOURNAL OF CHRISTIANITY
  Jul'40:144

JOURNAL OF EDUCATION
  May'37:101

JUSTICE
  Jul'34:159
  Aug'34:174

JUSTIN MARTYR
  Sep'37:197

K.

K., A. D.
  Letter. Jun'40:144

KENTUCKY, MEETING AT COOPER'S RUN
  Sep'38:210

KENTUCKY, TOUR IN
  Mar'40:63

KENTUCKY, VISIT TO
  May'35:109
  Jun'35:123
  Oct'40:217

KEYS OF THE KINGDOM
  Nov'38:241

KING, E.
  Letter. Aug'41:180

KING JAMES TRANSLATION COMMITTEE
  Oct'38:218

KING, JULIA A.
  Letter. Sep'39:213

KING, SUSAN
  Obituary. Sep'39:213

KINGDOM OF HEAVEN
  May'34:97
  Jun'34:121

KINGDOMS OF EUROPE
  Aug'42:171

KINGDOMS, THE THREE
  Feb'40:41

KYES, ALVIN
  Letter. Apr'33:95

L.

LAFAYETTE SEMINARY
    Feb'35:45
    May'40:120

LANTHAM, C. N.
    Letter. Apr'34:93

LATHAM, THOMAS J.
    Letter. Mar'34:71
             Jun'40:140

LATIMER, J. B.
    Letter. May'42:115

LAVER OF REGENERATION
    Mar'32:60

LAW SCHOOLS
    Jul'32:168

LAYTON, P. S.
    Letter. Jul'39:161

LECTURE BY WILLIAM MILLER
    Aug'42:174

LEGION, OR TWELVE YEARS OBSERVATION AND
EXAMINATION OF MR. CAMPBELL'S THEORY AND
PRACTICE OF REFORMATION
    Nov'35:257

LESSONS ON GENESIS
    Feb'38:29

LET THEM ALONE
    Jun'35:128
    Aug'35:169

LETTER FROM A FATHER TO A SON
    Sep'40:212

LETTER FROM AN AFFECTIONATE BROTHER
    Jul'41:166

LETTER FROM A. R. TO ALONZO
    Jun'41:137

LETTER TO DR. PRESSLY
    Sep'41:193
    Nov'41:252

Dec'41:275
Jan'42:9

LETTERS
    Apr'41:92
    Jul'41:158

LEWIS, WILLIAM W.
    Letter. Apr'34:94

LEXINGTON, KENTUCKY, UNION MEETING AT
    Jun'41:127

LETTER ON SLAVERY
    Jun'35:136

LIBERATOR
    Jun'35:136,144
    Jul'35:150
    Aug'35:174
    Oct'35:238

LICENSING FOR RIGHTS OF MATRIMONY
    Aug'38:185

LIFE, CHRISTIAN
    May'39:97

LINES ENGRAVED ON ENTRANCE OF THE JEW'S
BURIAL GROUND, GLASGOW
    Nov'35:263

LIQUOR
    Sep'38:209
    Sep'40:212

LIQUOR SALES
    Aug'38:191

LITCH, J.
    Letter. Jul'42:155

LITERATURE, HEBREW
    Jun'33:126

LITTELL, A.
    Letter. Feb'34:46
             Feb'35:39

LOGIC OF ROMANISM
    Sep'35:208

LORD, JESUS, THE
  Jul'40:152

LORD'S DAY ABSENCES
  Mar'39:72

LORD'S PRAYER
  Mar'39:71

LOST TRIBES FOUND
  Mar'42:65

LOVE-FEAST
  Apr'41:90

LOVING OTHERS BETTER THAN OURSELVES
  Mar'39:68

LUCAS, MR., PRESIDENT OF PROTESTANT
METHODIST CONFERENCE
  Oct'38:231

LUCY, BROTHER
  Sep'32:214

LUKE VII
  Feb'40:47

LUMINARY, THE WESTERN
  Jan'33:4
  Mar'33:52
  Jun'33:129
  Sep'33:197

LYND, DISCOURSE BY S. W.
  Apr'38:94

LYND ON BAPTISM
  Oct'33:217
  Nov'33:241,247
  Dec'33:265
  Feb'34:29
  Apr'34:82
  May'34:110

MAHOMET, AND THE POPES, DATES OF
  May'38:106

MAHONING ASSOCIATION OF 1830, CIRCULAR
LETTER FOR THE
  Feb'32:40

MALEDICTION, OR CURSE, THE
  Jul'38:164

MAN, SPIRIT OF
  May'37:117

MAN, THE GREATEST
  Jul'40:156

MANUSCRIPTS, DISCOVERY OF INTERESTING
  Oct'34:240

MARRIAGE
  Dec'32:265,269
  Jun'40:140

MARTIN, J. G.
  Letter. Sep'33:214

MARTIN, WARNICK
  Letter. Dec'35:283

MASONS
  Aug'38:182

MATERIAL SYSTEM, TEMPORARY NATURE OF THE
  Jul'40:156

MATHES, J. M.
  Letter. Aug'37:167
           Jun'42:127

MATTHEWS, JAMES M.
  Letter. Aug'38:192
           Jul'39:161
           Oct'41:232

MATTHEWS, THOMAS J.
  Letter. Aug'33:192

MAYSLICK, KENTUCKY, MEETING AT
  Jun'32:139

MEAD, EDWARD
  Letter. May'35:108

MEDICAL SCHOOLS
  Jul'32:168

MEDICAL SOCIETY, CONSTITUTION OF THE
PEOPLE'S
  Aug'42:170

MEDICINE, NEW ERA IN
  Aug'42:169

MEEKNESS
  Dec'39:280

MEETING AT BURLINGTON, KENTUCKY
  Jul'39:167

MEETING AT CARTHAGE, OHIO
  Oct'33:238
  Aug'40:192
  Sep'40:216
  Sep'41:216

MEETING AT COOPER'S RUN, KENTUCKY
  Sep'38:210
  Jun'41:140

MEETING AT DAYTON, OHIO
  Aug'42:190

MEETING AT GEORGETOWN, KENTUCKY
  Apr'38:87

MEETING AT HARRODSBURGH, KENTUCKY
  May'40:100

MEETING AT LEXINGTON, KENTUCKY
  Jun'41:127

MEETING AT MAYSLICK, KENTUCKY
  Jun'32:139

MEETING AT MURFREESBORO, TENNESSEE
  Jun'32:142

MEETING AT NORTH MIDDLETOWN, KENTUCKY
  Apr'38:85

MISTAKES CORRECTED
Oct'37:168

MITCHELL, JAMES
Letter. Oct'33:237

MITCHELL'S AMERICAN SYSTEM OF
STANDARD SCHOOL GEOGRAPHY
Oct'41:238

MODESTY
Dec'39:281

MONROE, D.
Letter. Sep'39:206

MOODY, GEORGE
Letter. Nov'40:255

MOOKLAR, WILLIAM B.
Letter. Jun'42:141
Oct'42:239

MOORE, GABRIEL B.
Letter. May'34:115
Jul'34:164

MORGAN, DAVID
Letter. Aug'41:180

MORMON BIBLE
Jul'39:158
Jan'41:17
Feb'41:42
Mar'41:62
May'41:111
Jun'41:132

MORMON RESOLUTION
Sep'33:215

MORMONISM
Oct'38:226
Feb'42:32

MORMONS
Jul'41:165

MORNING AND EVENING PRAYER
May'40:109

MORNING PRAYER
Aug'41:191

MORNING WATCH, THE
Feb'38:47
Aug'38:185

MORRIS, THOMAS A.
Letter. Aug'34:174

MORTON, WILLIAM
Letter. Jan'37:20

MOSAIC RELIGION
May'33:106

MOSES, THE THIRD PROPHECY OF
Oct'32:224

MOTHER'S INJUNCTION ON PRESENTING HER
SON WITH A BIBLE
Oct'34:240

MOTHER'S LOVE, A
Nov'34:262

MULLINS, SAMUEL G.
Letter. Jul'40:146

MURFREESBORO, TENNESSEE
Jun'32:142

MUSEUM, YOUNG LADIES'
Apr'40:96

MUSIC, SACRED
Aug'38:186
Feb'39:48
Aug'39:191
Dec'39:265

MYSTERIES EXPLAINED IN A SERMON
Oct'35:236

Mc.

McCALL, J. R.
   Letter. Sep'33:211
             Jan'35:22

McCANN, J. W.
   Letter. Sep'33:214

McCLENAHAN, WILLIAM
   Letter. Jan'34:22

McELROY, JAMES
   Letter. Feb'32:47
             Apr'33:94

McGEE, JOHN
   Letter. Dec'33:283

McNEELY, CYRUS
   Letter. Apr'32:95
             Dec'33:283

N.

NEW TRANSLATION OF THE OLD TESTAMENT
  Jun'33:137

NEW VERSION OF THE OLD TESTAMENT
SCRIPTURES
  Aug'32:169
  Sep'32:195
  Dec'32:274

NEW YORK, CHURCH OF CHRIST IN
  Jul'38:155

NEWS
  Jun'38:143

NEWS FROM THE CHURCHES
  Jan'39:23

NON-GOVERNMENT MEN
  Jul'41:146

NON-PRAYING PROFESSORS
  Apr'40:90

NON-PROGRESSIVE CHURCHES
  Apr'40:88

NON-WORSHIP FAMILIES
  Apr'40:89

NORTH WESTERN PASSAGE
  Jul'40:168

NOTE
  Oct'32:217
  Dec'32:265
  Mar'33:50
  Jul'33:153
  Oct'33:229,233
  Nov'33:241
  Feb'34:37,44
  Sep'34:204
  Mar'35:49
  Apr'35:77
  Dec'35:280

NOTE BY D. G.
  Jun'33:144

NORTHERN REFORMER, THE
  May'37:100

NORTON, J.
  Letter. Dec'42:282

NOTICE
  Jan'34:20
  Feb'38:48
  Jul'38:168
  Mar'41:72

NUT FOR GEOLOGISTS, A
  Aug'40:188

O.

OBEDIENCE, POSITIVE AND MORAL
  May'42:101
  Jun'42:134
  Jul'42:148
  Aug'42:173
  Oct'42:233
  Dec'42:270

OBITUARY ONTICE OF SISTERS
YANELY AND FOSTER
  Jul'37:152

OBJECT AND PRINCIPLE
  Aug'41:180

OBSERVATION
  Oct'35:221,235

OBSERVATIONS ON THE DISCOURSE OF
BROTHER HALL
  Sep'40:206

ODD FELLOWS SOCIETY
  Aug'38:192

OFFICE I STUDY IN, THE
  Jan'42:11
  Feb'42:27
  Mar'42:49
  May'42:106
  Jan'42:131

OHIO MEDICAL COLLEGE
  Aug'35:192

OHIO, TO THE BRETHREN IN
  Aug'40:187

O'KANE, JOHN
  Letter. Dec'39:284

OLNEY KITE, THE
  May'35:120

OMNIPOTENCE OF GOD
  May'40:108

OMNIPRESENCE GOD'S
  May'40:109

ON READING THE SCRIPTURES
  May'32:114
  Jul'32:161

ONE OBJECTION ANSWERED
  Dec'41:281

ORACLES, ON COMMITTING THE
  Jul'33:154
  Aug'33:171

ORANGE, DANIEL
  Letter. Feb'42:44

ORDER
  Jul'40:161

ORDER AND DISCIPLINE OF APOSTOLIC
CHURCHES
  Sep'38:215

ORGANIZATION
  Dec'42:265

ORTHODOX, SHORT SERMON FOR THE
  Nov'41:260

OUR COURSE
  Nov'40:241

OWEN, E.
  Letter. Dec'33:284

OWEN, ROBERT DALE
  Apr'32:76

OWEN, THOMAS
  Letter. Feb'42:45

PADGET, GEORGE W.
  Letter. Jul'42:168

PALESTINE, ARABIA AND
  Dec'39:268

PALESTINE, CONVERSION OF THE JEWS IN
  Apr'40:84

PALLADIUM, THE CHRISTIAN
  Jun'41:144

PAPISTRY
  Mar'39:65

PARABLES, THOUGHTS ON
  Feb'34:25
  May'34:98

PAST YEAR, THE
  Jan'40:15

PATRIOTISM
  Nov'40:254

PAUL BEFORE AGRIPPA
  Oct'41:240

PAULUS, EPISTLE OF
  Feb'33:63

PAXTON, BROTHER
  Letter. Apr'32:95

PAYNE, W. P.
  Letter. Apr'34:93
           Oct'41:223
           Feb'42:41

PEPPER, BROTHER
  Letter. Jan'33:22

PERFECTION
  Jan'40:5,6
  Feb'40:25,26,28
  Mar'40:49
  Apr'40:77,82
  May'40:102,104
  Jun'40:128
  Jul'40:145,148
  Aug'40:184,185

Sep'40:193,203,205
Oct'40:225,227
Dec'40:265,272
Jan'41:11
Feb'41:39
Mar'41:61
May'41:115
Jun'41:130
Jul'41:152
Aug'41:175
Jan'42:7
May'42:104
Jun'42:124
Jul'42:153

PERFECTION OF THE CONSCIENCE
  Jul'39:145

PERKINS, LUCINDA
  Obituary. Oct'41:230

PERSECUTION OF THE JEWS
  Oct'40:235

PERSECUTION, RELIGIOUS
  May'42:112

PERSONAL DEVOTION
  Mar'39:62

PHENOMENON
  Feb'34:44

PHENOMENON, EXTRAORDINARY
  Nov'42:250

PHILEMON, THE EPISTLE OF PAUL TO
  Apr'35:82

PHILOSOPHY OF RELIGION
  Jan'32:22
  Mar'32:63
  Jun'32:128
  Oct'32:233

PICKETT, ALBERT
  Letter. Aug'33:192

PINKERTON, L. L.
  Letter. Jul'39:162
          Sep'39:206
          Oct'40:236
          Oct'41:231,233

PINKERTON, W.
  Letter. Apr'41:95
          Dec'41:282

PITT, DORSEY
  Letter. Jan'33:22

PITTSBURGH, PENNSYLVANIA, MEETING AT
  Jul'39:167

PITTSBURGH, PUBLIC MEETING AT
  Sep'38:204

PLANTE, THE CONDEMNED
  Jun'42:136

PLEA FOR A NEW VERSION OF THE
OLD TESTAMENT SCRIPTURES
  Aug'32:169
  Sep'32:195
  Dec'32:274

PLEA, PROGRESS OF THE GREAT AND GOOD
  Mar'41:69

POETRY
  Apr'33:93

POINDEXTER, BROTHER
  Apr'33:94

POLITICAL EXECUTIVE GOVERNMENT
  Oct'32:240

POMEROY, JAMES
  Letter. Mar'40:71
          Nov'40:259

PONTIUS PILATE AT VIENNE
  Nov'39:241

POOL, WILLIAM F.
  Letter. Oct'41:233
          Aug'42:189

POOR, ELOQUENT PLEA FOR THE
  Jul'42:156

POOR, THE
  Jan'38:7

POPERY, THOUGHTS ON
  May'37:113

POPES, DATES OF MAHOMET, AND THE
  May'38:106

POPULAR CONVERSION
  Dec'33:270

POPULAR HILL FEMALE SEMINARY, KENTUCKY
  Aug'40:192

PRATT, JOHN JR.
  Letter. Sep'34:216

PRAYER, MORNING
  Aug'41:191

PRAYER, MORNING AND EVENING
  May'40:109

PREACHER, THE
  Jan'38:22

PREACHERS, CALLED AND SENT
  Jun'41:126

PREACHERS, SCHOOL OF THE
  Jan'38:14

PREACHERS WANTED
  Jun'41:144

PREACHERS AND PERIODICALS
  Apr'42:87

PREACHING AND TEACHING
  Apr'42:89

PREACHING EXPERIENCES
  Jul'39:154

PREDESTINARIAN AND HIS FRIEND, DIALOGUE
BETWEEN A
  Apr'37:84

PREFACE
  Feb'33:25
  Jan'38:1

Q.

R.

R., C.
  Letter. Sep'39:208

R., O.
  Letter. Nov'40:259

R., T.
  Letter. Sep'39:209

R., Z.
  Letter. Oct'41:226

RAINS, AYLETT
  Letter. Jun'32:143
           Apr'33:95
           May'33:103
           Oct'35:233

RAINS, SELECTIONS BY AYLETT
  Jun'37:6

READ, JOHN
  Letter. Mar'34:71
           Aug'38:192

REASONS FOR EMBRACING THE ANCIENT
GOSPEL
  Nov'32:252

RECANTATION OF A CLERGYMAN
  Oct'33:229

RECEIPTS FOR CHRISTIAN
  Apr'37:96
  May'37:116
  Sep'37:183

RECEIPTS FOR EVANGELIST
  Mar'38:72
  May'38:121
  Jul'38:168
  Sep'38:217
  May'39:120
  Jul'39:168
  Sep'39:216
  Feb'40:48

RECEIPTS FOR GOSPEL RESTORED
  Mar'38:72
  May'38:121
  Jul'38:168
  Sep'38:217

REED, ALEXANDER
  Letter. Sep'39:207
           Dec'40:282,283
           Apr'42:93

REED, BROTHER (MONROE COUNTY, OHIO)
  Letter. Sep'32:215

REFLECTIONS ON THE DEATH OF A BROTHER
  Aug'32:191

REFLECTIONS ON THE SEASON
  Jan'35:1

REFORM, PROGRESS OF
  Feb'34:46
  Mar'34:71

REFORMATION
  Jan'32:19
  Mar'35:61
  Apr'35:90
  Aug'35:171
  Sep'35:193
  Nov'35:151

REFORMATION PERFECTED
  Jan'41:22

REFORMATION PUBLICATIONS
  Aug'39:189

REFORMATION, THE ROMISH CHURCH SINCE THE
  May'41:100

REFORMER, BISHOP
  Mar'40:57
  Apr'40:90
  Jun'40:133

REFORMER, THE HERETIC DETECTOR AND THE
  Jul'37:146

REFORMERS, SELF-STYLED
  Oct'38:225

REGENERATION
  Mar'42:52

REGENERATION, LAVER OF
  Mar'32:60

REID, G. C.
Letter. Nov'40:261

REID, WALKER
Letter. Feb'32:47

RELIGION
Oct'37:190
Jan'38:8

RELIGION AND THE REIGNING SOVEREIGNS
OF EUROPE
May'32:120

RELIGION, BENEFITING FROM OTHERS IN
Mar'39:69

RELIGION, EVIDENCE OF
Aug'39:192

RELIGION IN THE HEART
Aug'38:183

RELIGION, INSTITUTES OF
Feb'40:39

RELIGION, NATURE AND
Mar'39:69

RELIGION, PHILOSOPHY OF
Jan'32:22
Mar'32:63
Jun'32:128

RELIGION, PROSPECTUS OF
Jul'39:149

RELIGIOUS DENOMINATIONS
Mar'32:72

RELIGIOUS DIVISION
May'37:101

RELIGIOUS PERSECUTION
May'42:112

RELIGIOUS PRINCIPLES, CONCERNING
CULTIVATION OF
Jan'38:6

RELIGIOUS RIDDLES
Jun'40:139

RELIGIOUS STATISTICS
Oct'40:240

REMAINS OF JAPHET
Jun'32:132

REMARKS ON GENERAL MEETINGS
Aug'34:181

REMISSION AND THE HOLY SPIRIT
Jan'33:4

REMISSION OF SINS, BAPTISM FOR THE
Dec'40:278

RENEAU, ISAAC T.
Letter. Sep'39:207
Feb'40:46
Jul'41:163
Oct'41:231
Feb'42:40

RENEAU, J. T.
Letter. Jan'39:24

REPENTANCE
May'32:100

REPROVER
Letter. Nov'34:260

RESE, FRED
Letter. Jul'33:162

RESIGNATION
Dec'39:281

RESOURCES OF THE EUROPEAN POWERS
Apr'33:96

RESTORATION OF THE ANCIENT GOSPEL
Jan'33:1,15
Mar'33:50
Apr'33:88
May'33:97
Jul'33:160

RESTORATION OF THE TRUE GOSPEL
Aug'38:180

RESTORERS OF THE ANCIENT GOSPEL, THE
PROFESSED, -AN ANSWER
Jun'34:122
Jul'34:153

RESURRECTION, THE
Oct'41:220

RESURRECTION, THE END AND PURPOSE
TO BE EFFECTED BY THE
May'33:112

RESURRECTION, VISION OF THE
Jan'40:24

REVELATION, A FUNDAMENTAL ARGUMENT FOR
A DIVINE
Apr'38:83

REVIEW OF D's FIFTH ESSAY ON THE
HOLY SPIRIT
Aug'34:177

REVIEW OF GRIMKE'S ADDRESS
Feb'32:37
Mar'32:67

REYNOLDS, BROTHER
Letter. Sep'32:214
Jan'33:22

REYNOLDS, WILLIAM P.
Letter. Aug'33:191

RICE, R. C.
Letter. Aug'41:189

RICHARDSON, ROBERT
Letter. Jul'32:167
Jan'33:21
Apr'34:95,96
Jul'41:162

RICKETS, R. C.
Letter. Oct'35:240
Apr'37:96
Jul'37:152

RIGHT IMPROVEMENT OF LIFE
Feb'42:48

ROACH, DR.
Letter. Sep'33:214

ROBERT, DALE OWEN
Apr'32:76

ROBERT HALL OF LEICESTER IN THE PULPIT
Jun'40:138

ROBERT, LOUIS J. D.
Letter. Jun'34:142

ROBERTS, U. M.
Letter. Sep'34:212

ROBBINS, SAMUEL
Letter. Jul'39:161

ROGERS, ELIZA
Obituary. Feb'41:46

ROGERS, ELLEN
Obituary. Jul'39:165

ROGERS, I.
Letter. Sep'33:213

ROGERS, JOHN
Jul'35:163

ROGERS, JOHN
Letter. May'32:112
Sep'33:213
Jan'37:11
Apr'37:93
May'37:117
Jul'39:165

ROGERS, JOHN AND FATHER STONE
May'42:102

ROGERS, W.
Letter. Sep'33:214

ROMAN CATHOLIC DISCUSSION
Jan'37:18

ROMANISM, LOGIC OF
Sep'35:208

ROME AND JERUSALEM
Oct'39:228
Jul'41:172

ROMISH CHURCH SINCE THE REFORMATION, THE
May'41:100

ROSS, SAMUEL
Letter. Mar'35:65

RUDULPH, JOHN
Letter. Apr'34:90

RUNYAN, ASA
   Letter. Mar'32:71
            Jun'32:142
            Jan'34:23
            May'34:116
            Jan'35:23
            May'38:119

RUSSELL, BROTHER
   Letter. Jun'32:143

RUSSIA, THE DESIGNS OF
   Nov'39:250

SCIENCE, SYNOPSIS OF
  Feb'42:31

SCIENCE, TABLE OF
  Mar'42:29

SCOTT, SERMON BY SIR WALTER
  Oct'35:224
  Nov'35:244

SCOTT, WALTER
  Letter. Jan'32:17
          Jun'33:142
          Aug'33:191
          Nov'33:256
          Dec'33:282
          Mar'34:72
          May'34:113,119
          Jun'34:139
          Jul'34:160,168
          Sep'34:213,215
          Oct'34:234
          Nov'34:251
          Feb'35:43
          Mar'35:65,69
          Apr'35:80,86
          Jun'35:135,136,141
          Sep'35:205
          May'37:109
          Dec'38:267,268,270,272,275,
          278,281,287,288
          Jan'39:23,24
          Mar'39:72
          Sep'39:207,208
          Nov'39:259
          Mar'40:71
          May'40:113
          Jun'40:141
          Oct'40:239
          Nov'40:258
          Dec'40:283
          Mar'41:71
          Sep'41:215
          Jun'42:140
          Nov'42:260

SCRANTON, WILLIAM A.
  Letter. Aug'33:188

SCRANTON, W. C.
  Letter. Dec'42:276

SCRATTON, BROTHER
  Letter. Sep'32:215

SCRIBES, THE
  Sep'35:201

SCRIPTURES, FALSIFICATION OF THE
  Jul'33:164

SCRIPTURES, GENUINNESS OF THE
  Aug'38:181

SCRIPTURES IN COMMON SCHOOLS, STUDY (
THE HOLY
  Sep'38:200,201

SCRIPTURES, ON READING THE
  May'32:114
  Jul'32:161

SCRIPTURES, STUDY OF THE
  Jun'38:135
  Aug'38:171
  Jan'39:18
  May'39:112

SCRIPTURES, THE
  Aug'41:189

SCRUTATOR
  Letter. Nov'34:262

SECOND COMING OF CHRIST
  Jun'34:134
  Jul'34:145
  Aug'34:169
  Oct'34:219
  Nov'34:241
  Feb'35:33
  Mar'35:55
  May'35:114
  Jul'41:147
  Oct'41:228
  Nov'41:249,254
  Dec'41:269,277,281
  Jan'42:5
  May'42:97
  Jun'42:121
  Jul'42:150
  Oct'42:234

SECOND DEATH
  Aug'38:190

SECREST, J.
  Letter. Oct'32:238

SECTS AMONG THE CHRISTIANS
  Apr'40:73

SEMON, E. W.
  Letter. May'35:109

SELECTIONS BY AYLETT RAINS
  Jan'37:6

SELF-IMPROVEMENT, HINTS ON
  Aug'41:183

SEMINARIES, THEOLOGICAL
  Jul'32:168

SEMINARY, LAFAYETTE
  May'40:120

SERMON, A SHORT
  Aug'41:175

SERMON BY SIR WALTER SCOTT
  Oct'35:224
  Nov'35:244

SHANNON'S INNAUGURAL ADDRESS, PRESIDENT
  Jun'41:143

SHEPHERD, USELESS
  Apr'40:89

SHOCKLEY, ABIGAIL
  Obituary. Jul'35:168

SHORT, NEWTON
  Letter. Apr'37:93

SHORT SERMON, A
  Aug'41:175

SHORT SERMON FOR THE ORTHODOX, A
  Nov'41:260

SIGNS OF THE TIMES
  Jul'41:147
  Oct'41:238
  Sep'42:205
  Dec'42:275

SIMPLIFICATION
  Feb'34:34
  Mar'34:49

SIN AND ITS CURE
  Jul'35:165
  Oct'38:225

SIN, DEAD IN
  Oct'37:171

SLAVERY
  Jan'35:17
  Feb'35:39
  Jun'35:136

SLEIGH, DR.
  Sep'35:213

SLEIGH, TO EDITOR OF EVANGELIST
  Oct'34:225
  Nov'34:249

SLEIGH'S PAMPHLET, OBSERVATIONS ON DR.
  Sep'34:193

SMITH, CAREY
  Letter. Feb'35:42

SOCIAL IMPROVEMENT
  Jul'38:162

SOCIETY AND RELIGION, NATURE
  May'35:116
  Jul'35:152

SOCRATES, DEATH OF
  Dec'39:272

SONG, A
  Sep'37:192

SOUL, THE
  Aug'41:191

SOWARD, A.
  Letter. Jun'32:143

SPALDING, D.
  Letter. Nov'42:262

SPIRIT.-NO. V, ESSAYS ON THE HOLY
  Aug'34:175

SPIRIT OF MAN
  May'37:117

SPIRIT, REVIEW OF D'S FIFTH ESSAY
ON THE HOLY
Aug'34:177

SPIRIT, UNITY OF THE
Feb'40:36
Apr'40:79

SPIRITUAL INFLUENCE
Sep'40:194,195,206
Dec'40:267

STAMPS, BROTHER
Letter. Sep'32:215

STANDARD, FROM THE
Jul'32:165

STANDIFORD, W.
Letter. Jan'39:24

STARRY HEAVENS, CONTEMPLATION OF THE
Mar'42:61

STARTING POINT, THE
Oct'40:233

STATE-SYSTEM, THE
Feb'-Mar'37:25

STATISTICS OF THE UNITED STATES
Jun'40:140

STATISTICS, RELIGIOUS
Oct'40:240

STEELE, BROTHER
Letter. Apr'33:95

STEELE, JOHN
Letter. Oct'33:236

STEELE, O. C.
Letter. Jun'37:152
Mar'39:72

STILES AGAIN, MR.
Oct'37:181

STONE AND BROTHER ROGERS, FATHER
May'42:102

STONE, BARTON W.
Letter. Mar'32:71
Nov'39:259

STONE, D. WINDER AND FATHER
May'42:110

STONE, ELDER BARTON W.
Nov'41:248

STRICCLE, A. S.
Letter. Jan'39:23

STRICKLE, E. A.
Letter. Jul'34:165

STRONG, WILLIAM H.
Letter. Oct'34:236
Jan'35:4

STUDY OF THE HOLY SCRIPTURES IN
COMMON SCHOOLS
Sep'38:200,201

STUDY OF THE SCRIPTURES
Jun'38:135
Aug'38:171
Jan'39:18
May'39:112

STYLES, JOS. C.
Letter. Sep'37:186,189

SUBSCRIBERS, TO
Jun'35:144
Nov'40:264
Oct'41:239
Oct'42:240

SUCCESS OF THE GOSPEL
Jan'37:20
Apr'37:93
Oct'37:176
Jan'38:24

SUCCESSION OF WORLDS
Jan'38:3
Feb'38:33,44
Apr'38:73
Aug'38:174

SUFFERINGS, PRIMITIVE
Feb'32:31

SUNDERIES
  Mar'33:59
  May'33:116
  Jul'39:153

SWEARING
  Jan'32:5

SWEENY, L. S.
  Letter. Jan'37:21

SYRIA, THE CHRISTIANS OF
  Aug'41:171

SYSTEM, TEMPERARY NATURE OF THE MATERIAL
  Jul'40:156

TABLE OF GOVERNMENT
Nov'32:264

TABLE OF SCIENCE
Feb'42:29

TAIT, JOHN
Letter. Sep'32:215
Dec'38:287

TALENT AND TACT
May'35:106

TALENT, GENIUS AND
May'35:107

TAYLOR, SAMUEL
Letter. May'34:114
Jul'34:164

TAYLOR, THOMAS
Letter. May'42:114

TEACHERS, TO
Mar'39:72

TEMPORARY NATURE OF THE MATERIAL
SYSTEM
Jul'40:156

TEN-HORNED BEAST, THE
Apr'41:80
May'41:102

THEATRE, THE
Jun'34:131

THEOLOGICAL SEMINARIES
Jul'32:168

THEORIES ON THE MILLENNIUM
May'42:100

THEORY OF REFORMATION PERFECTED, THE
Jan'41:22

THIRD PROPHECY OF MOSES
Oct'32:224

THOMAS, J.
Letter. Dec'33:263
Jul'41:159

THOMAS, JOHN, AND A. CAMPBELL, DIFFI
TIES BETWEEN
Mar'39:67

THOMPSON, BROTHER
Letter. Sep'33:213

THOMPSON, J.
Letter. Aug'41:180

THOUGHTS ON THE PARABLES
Feb'34:25
May'34:98

THREE DIVINE INSTITUTIONS
Jan'32:13
Feb'32:34
Apr'32:89
Aug'32:184
Oct'32:222

THY WILL BE DONE
Mar'42:72

TOBACCO CHEWING
May'38:116

TOTAL ABSTINENCE
Jul'42:157

TOTAL HEREDITARY DEPRAVITY
Jun'33:133
Jul'34:151

TRIUMPHANT CONFRONTATION
Jun'39:121

TROWBRIDGE, BROTHER
May'32:119

TRUE DELIGHT
Aug'41:188

TRUMAN, RD.
Letter. Jun'40:143

TURNER, J. M.
Letter. Nov'40:257

U.

V.

W.

WADSWORTH, MR.
  Mar'38:72

WAITE, DANIEL
  Letter. May'35:118

WALLIS, JAMES
  Letter. Sep'37:194
          Jan'40:20
          Dec'42:283

WATERFORD, CHURCH OF CHRIST IN
  Jul'38:160

WATTS, G. W.
  Letter. May'42:117

WEAVER, T.
  Letter. Aug'41:180

WELSH, BROTHER
  Letter. Apr'32:95

WELLY, G.
  Letter. Aug'39:191

WESTERN ACADEMICIAN
  May'37:100

WESTERN FARMER AND GARDNER, THE
  Oct'41:237

WESTERN LUMINARY, THE
  Jan'33:4
  Mar'33:52
  Jun'33:129
  Sep'33:197

WESTERN RESERVE, VISIT TO PITTSBURG
AND THE
  Jan'38:8

WHARTON, WILLIAM H.
  Letter. Jun'34:132
          Jul'35:167

WHIP, PETER
  Letter. Mar'41:72

WHITFIELD, ROBERT H.
  Letter. Jan'37:22

WILLIAMS, F.
  Letter. Apr'33:95
          Feb'35:42

WILLIAMS, GEORGE W.
  Letter. May'38:118

WILLIAMS, JOEL P.
  Letter. Jun'40:146

WILLIAMS, MILO G.
  Letter. Aug'33:192

WINANS, ANSWER TO
  Sep'33:209
  Nov'33:256
  Feb'34:37
  Mar'34:64
  May'34:113
  Nov'40:258
  Nov'42:260

WINANS, M.
  Letter. Jun'33:141
           Sep'33:208
           Oct'33:237
           Nov'33:255
           Dec'33:282
           Mar'34:67
           Apr'34:96
           May'34:113
           Jun'34:130
           Dec'34:278
           Apr'35:96
           May'35:117
           Jun'35:133
           Aug'35:190
           Apr'38:96
           Oct'39:237
           Jan'40:22
           Sep'40:215
           Nov'40:258
           Dec'40:282
           Feb'42:43,45
           Jun'42:140
           Nov'42:258

WINDER, D.
  Letter. Jun'42:123
           Aug'42:188

WINDER, D., AND FATHER STONE
  May'42:110

WINN, WILLIS H.
  Letter. Jul'40:146

WIRT, CATHARINE C.
  Letter. Jan'35:7

WIRT, THE LAST ILLNESS OF MR. WILLIAM
  Jan'35:7

WIVES, TO
  Feb'41:39

WOMAN, BUSY
  Mar'39:72

WOMEN, MEN AND
  Jul'41:167

WOOD, T.
  Letter. Jul'35:164

WOODWARD COLLEGE, CINCINATTI
  Oct'38:235

WOOLEN, JOHN M.
  Letter. Feb'35:42

WORD TO THE WISE, A
  Aug'38:174

WORLDS, OF A SUCCESSION OF
  Jan'38:3
  Feb'38:33,44
  Apr'38:73
  Aug'38:174

WORSHIP, LATE FOR
  Mar'39:72

WORTHINGTON, IN MEMORY OF MARY
  Nov'39:256

WRIGHT, A.
  Letter. Sep'33:213

WRIGHT, JOSHUA
  Letter. Nov'40:257

Y.

Y., P. G.
  Letter. Feb'35:47

YEAR, THE PAST
  Jan'40:15

YOUNG LADIES' MUSEUM
  Apr'40:96

YOUNG, WILLIS W.
  Letter. Sep'32:214